HOW WE ALL SWIFTLY

How We All Swiftly

THE FIRST SIX BOOKS

Don Coles

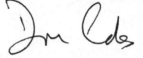

SIGNAL EDITIONS IS AN IMPRINT OF VÉHICULE PRESS

Published with the generous assistance of The Canada Council for the
Arts and the Book Publishing Industry Development Program of the
Department of Canadian Heritage.

The publisher would like to thank The Porcupine's Quill for its assistance
in realizing this project.

Signal Editions editor: Carmine Starnino
Cover design: David Drummond
Photo of author: Danielle Schaub
Set in Minion by Simon Garamond
Printed by Marquis Book Printing Inc.

Printed on 100% post-consumer recycled paper

LIBRARY AND ARCHIVES CANADA CATALOGUING IN PUBLICATION DATA

Coles, Don
How we all swiftly : the first six books Don Coles
Poems.
ISBN 1-55065-197-8

I. Title.

PS8555.O439H69 2005   c811'.54   C2005-904605-8

Published by Véhicule Press, Montréal, Québec, Canada
www.vehiculepress.com

Distribution in Canada by LitDistCo
orders@litdistco.ca
Distributed in the U.S. by Independent Publishers Group
www.ipgbook.com

Printed in Canada.

to

Dennis Lee, who got this show on the road an unforgotten 30 years ago, and

to

John Metcalf, whose exuberant confidence in the show's every performance filled and still fills me, and

to

Carmine Starnino, who will be the Sainte-Beuve of this land before he knows it,

my thanks

Contents

Introduction

I

BEFORE THE PUBLICATION of this book, Don Coles had published eight volumes of verse (nine, if one counts *Someone Has Stayed in Stockholm* [1994], his selected poems published in England) that extend over a quarter of a century from *Sometimes All Over* (1975) to *Kurgan* (2000). The time is clearly ripe not only for a reprinting of his earlier verse but also for a detailed consideration of this oeuvre, which has not received the critical attention it deserves, though mention should be made of the special edition of *Arc*, "Don Coles at 75, *Arc* at 25," published in 2003. The reason for this comparative neglect is not, however, difficult to discover. Coles is a poet of obvious quality, but one who does not fit easily into the accepted patterns of Canadian literary history. He is, in many respects, a loner. As Cary Fagan has pointed out in a useful article-cum-interview: "Unlike some of the poets of his generation, he has not become a performer or a public character, nor has he waved the banners of liberation or Canadian nationalism to win our attention. Instead, he has simply written his poems and published them without fanfare" (22).

But precisely who are "the poets of his generation"? Coles was born in 1928, but did not publish his first volume until 1975, when he was forty-seven. After completing his university education (B.A. and M.A. Toronto, M.A. Cambridge) by 1955, at a time when most of his writer-contemporaries would be beginning to publish their early work, Coles, who had already spent two years in England, spent another ten years wandering around continental Europe, not returning to Canada until 1965. True, he had begun writing in Europe, but this involved the production of several unsuccessful plays and abortive novels; he realized extraordinarily late that, if he had any talent for writing, it was as a poet (though he has recently displayed an impressive albeit late mastery of fiction with the publication of *Doctor Bloom's Story* in 2004). By his own testimony, he didn't begin to write poetry until "around 1966 or '67" (Carbert 118), and it was another eight years or so before *Sometimes All Over* eventually appeared. His, then, is an unusual case, and, given the historical period in which it occurred, it had unusual repercussions. The point is best made, perhaps, by observing that, while technically a poet of the generation of James Reaney, D. G. Jones, and Jay Macpherson, and while the new Canadian poets when he began to write were Margaret Atwood, Pat Lane, and Michael Ondaatje, he made his poetic début in the company of Robert Kroetsch (as a poet), Daphne Marlatt, and Christopher Dewdney.

I suggest that a main reason for Coles' somewhat ambiguous position as a Canadian poet is to be explained by these biographical circumstances and their subsequent effects. First, he began working out his creative destiny in Europe rather than in North America, and within a curious hiatus between two literary-historical periods and two poetic modes. Thus he is old enough to have lived his formative years in a cultural atmosphere in which high modernism (Pound, Eliot, etc.) was still in place but showing signs of decline. Although he may have derived from these writers his deep-seated respect for cultural monuments of the past, he did not find them poetically congenial. "I can feel the odd fondness for Pound," he has remarked, "but Eliot was someone I was over-exposed to in university and never have felt warmth for" (Carbert 120).[1] In addition, the poets he was reading at this time had begun reacting not only against the modernists but against "the inflated Dylan Thomas-ish sort of Fifties poetry" (Carbert 120), while Coles' own instinct took him elsewhere to modes of writing that were, in some respects, more traditional. These included what he has called, when reviewing a book of poems by Christopher Wiseman back in 1982, "the Hardy-Larkin line of descent, not much acknowledged in these parts, yet one which I commend" ("Hardy-Larkin" 36).

Moreover, there were other complicating factors. Inspiring and crucial as his "wander-years" may have been, the period from the mid-fifties to the mid-sixties was, one might think, a little too late for such Hemingwayesque ventures, and he returned to a very different Canada: the Canada of Expo and the beginnings of an aggressive nationalism. For good or ill, the cultural lure of Europe had faded: rightly or wrongly, the younger poets, if they looked abroad at all (many of them felt the urgent need to concentrate on Canada and their own roots), turned their sights south of the border rather than east across the Atlantic. It was, as they say, a different ball-game.

As a result, Coles found himself in a unique but anomalous position. Many attitudes and approaches that might have seemed fresh and challenging in the fifties, and even the early sixties, were tame, even quaintly old-fashioned by the 1970s. This was nowhere more evident than in the areas of sexual mores and literary explicitness, and the changes can be illustrated readily enough by reference to the love-poems that make up a considerable percentage of the contents of *Sometimes All Over*. The nature of this material might well lead us to forget that the volume was published by a man in his late forties, but its tone and language are different matters. Unimaginable as it may seem today, even a title like "Your Body Before Winter" could in some quarters have produced a *frisson* of excitement if it had been written and published when Coles was in his mid-twenties. It is instructive at this point to recall the opening lines of what is probably the best-known of these love-poems:

> It is a more than common privilege
> to be allowed to enter
> your body
>
> which is so unarguably
> whiter & warmer & softer
> than mine

(I quote from the original version, revised in this reprinting.) A reader of these lines in 1975 would, I think, have noticed first a seemingly outmoded dignity and reticence—shades of a romantic courtliness poets like Irving Layton and his followers had long since labelled, damningly though not necessarily justly, as prissy and "genteel."

Coles' poetic world, then, is one of divided allegiances, and it is in the attempted reconciling of various dichotomies—both in the age and in himself—that so much of the tension and effectiveness of his art resides. Here, for instance, is a remark he made to Cary Fagan in 1992: "What I want poetry to be about has to do with the kinds of things that Henry James and Flaubert talk about—the need for impersonality."[2] And two years later, to Michael Carbert, he spoke of a move in his own poetry "from a more personal to a less personal stance." The relation of the personal to the impersonal is certainly important for Coles, and it is a topic that will preoccupy him throughout his work. In the early poems about marriage, parents, and children (several of which I shall be discussing in the next section) the personal is decidedly prominent, but it is almost invariably offered as representative, not uniquely private. The particular instance is so treated that it will be recognized by readers as universal in its application. This applies also to a poem like "Landslides," which first appeared in *The Prinzhorn Collection* and concerns the poet's visits to his mother in a geriatric ward.[3] Deeply personal emotion, though undoubtedly present, is produced by a concentration on the mother rather than the speaker son, the whole experience offered to those who have experienced or will experience similar situations. Later, however, the relation between personal and impersonal becomes increasingly more complex, as the connections between art and the personal are explored in depth. As we shall see, Joseph Grebing's horrendous private predicament in "The Prinzhorn Collection" is itself presented, disturbingly, as an art-object; in *K. in Love* the personality of Franz Kafka and that of the poet become subtly interwoven, while in the later "Forests of the Mediaeval World" (in the volume of that title) a personal love-affair is juxtaposed—even enveloped—by the impersonality of the once-great forests.

Coles' views on poetry are conveniently summarized in an unusually polemical press-release produced by his publisher, Macmillan, when *The Prinzhorn Collection* appeared in 1982. In it Coles is quoted as making statements that constitute a poetic manifesto. Since this document is not readily accessible, I shall quote it at some length:

> It's my hope that my book will be one that can be read by a good many people who normally don't find poetry welcoming. Not that I picture my poetry as welcoming exactly!–but I think it is accessible to serious readers. I think there is something like a transferable content to it.

This is a subject that Coles returns to more than once. In the interview with Michael Carbert, he laments "the gap between poetry and the average reader" (120-121), a situation for which he lays much of the blame on Eliot. As a practising poet he is naturally concerned about the decline of poetry-reading—and poetry-buying—in the last twenty-five years or so. (Significantly, shortly after *The Prinzhorn Collection* appeared, Macmillan abandoned its poetry list.) It is tempting, of course, to point out that, while lamenting this development, Coles was writing more and more poems that drew heavily on literary and artistic allusions and references that were by no means familiar to general readers. But he would not recognize this as an inconsistency. "[A] poem that's accessible," he asserts, "does not *have* to be shallow or superficial or simpleminded" (Carbert 121).

The 1982 press-release continues as follows:

I have no respect or admiration for art that insists primarily on its "otherness," its remoteness from a recognizable human place, e.g. through an esoteric vocabulary, structural self-indulgence, or as is now commonplace in Canadian poetry, a contorted straining after extreme images—mutilations in every stanza, suicides and fetuses on facing pages; a posture which is, in these decades, embarrassingly derivative, so many Sylvia Plaths writ tiny, these homunculi Ted Hugheses.

This is a subject that still worries him ten years later: "I'm not interested in the huge spate of confessional poems that we've been inundated with," he told Fagan (22), though he is somewhat troubled by the confessional element in the just-published *Little Bird* (1991), a matter to which I shall return. Here again we are confronted with tensions that seem to pull him in two directions, and more are to be found in the *Prinzhorn* press-release. After taking his stand against the "embarrassingly derivative," and rejecting "open-field poetry" *en passant*, he goes on to complain about "innovation for its own sake in poetry; since it usually represents an attempt to disguise the fact that one has not been able to think of anything substantial to say." The same point is implied in the later Carbert interview when he criticizes some of his early published poems that he did not collect into the first volume: "These poems have some verbal interest perhaps but they didn't investigate much of anything" (118).

At this point we might legitimately ask: what does Coles himself offer that could be described as "something substantial to say"? Clearly, he is concerned about "transferable content" or what he calls, again in the *Prinzhorn* press-release, "a comprehensive and usable piece of content, maybe even a 'dark morsel of contemplation.'" Reviewers and commentators have not, in fact, found much difficulty in identifying his major themes—at least, those most prominent in his early verse. His most characteristic poems may be described as "temporal meditations" (in Susan Glickman's useful phrase [156]), and they tend to visit and revisit a narrow but rich range of subject-matter dominated by continual explorations of the relentless effects of time and the inevitable dislocations that these bring. This leads naturally to a focus on the relationships between parents and children—parents who have once been children, children who will eventually grow up to become parents themselves. It also leads to a fascination with photography, the art that has the capacity to freeze time and so to cross the awesome divide between "then" and "now." In addition, of course, there are the poems, more common in his later work, stimulated by works of art and literature that act as eloquent mediations between past and present. In brief, Coles is concerned with the human ramifications of the strange experience of living in time.

These are important but traditional topics that have been the subjects of countless poems through the ages. His choice of "transferable content" is certainly in no danger of leading to "innovation for its own sake," but how, one may be tempted to wonder, can Coles produce anything that is not pallidly conventional? The answer, of course, is that innovation, if fraught with danger so far as subject-matter is concerned, is essential in terms of treatment. In this respect phrases like "transferable content" and "usable piece of content" can be misleading in that they suggest an excessive emphasis on thematic issues. Coles is, however, too good a poet not to know that content and treatment are inseparable, that the intellectual content of any poem can only be meaningful if embodied in appropriate words and rhythms. Coles' poetry, like all legitimate poetry, depends for its effects on his command of all those literary devices that are subsumed under the term "style"; his capacity for poetic thought can only exist within a vibrant language. I now wish to focus on those stylistic qualities, as manifest in some of his most successful poems from his first two volumes, that make even Coles' early work so remarkable.

II

The relation between poetry, educated speech, and the contemporary vernacular has been a matter of controversy for centuries. One thinks immediately of Thomas Gray's "The language of the age is never the language of poetry" and of William Wordsworth's "language really used by men," or the uneasy friendship, strained by fundamentally opposed poetic assumptions and prosodic principles, between Robert Bridges (author of *The Testament of Beauty*) and Gerard Manley Hopkins. In Canadian poetry, we remember Raymond Souster and Irving Layton rebelling against the refined gentility of their poetic forebears, and the extraordinary way in which Al Purdy developed from his Carman-influenced early years into his individual and compelling demotic style—which, it should be acknowledged immediately, though suggesting an aggressive vernacular, itself constitutes a carefully wrought poetic diction.

Because he spent a number of impressionable early years in Europe, Coles became conscious, more than most of his Canadian contemporaries, of the importance of an established cultural tradition, and his mature verse is peppered with references drawing upon the art and writings of the past and the biographies of those who produced them. At the same time, he is acutely aware of the need to reflect current linguistic patterns and to reproduce the cadences of modern, living speech. His practical challenge has been twofold: to forge a poetic language that can contain his learned (though never "academic") attitudes within an acceptable colloquial tone, and to find a way of communicating subject-matter that draws upon the cultural experience and achievement of the past to a contemporary readership in the process, so it seems, of losing both its awareness of history and its ear for poetry.

It is my belief that Coles committed himself to a rigorously disciplined apprenticeship in the art of verse that can be discerned in his early poetry and leads ultimately to the assured rhythms and cadences of his mature writing. The following discussion will therefore place a heavy though not exclusive emphasis on technical matters, but it is important to insist at the outset that I am well aware that such matters should not be separated from what is being expressed. Like Coles, I know that any poetry worth writing (and writing about) ought to be, in the words of F. R. Leavis, both "the agent and vehicle of thought" (97). But technical poetic dexterity needs to be emphasized at this time. A poet's vision of life can only be conveyed in a distinctive and appropriate language, and in an age of countless specialized languages with their accompanying vocabularies—those of computers, the sciences, the professions, etc.—poets must create their own means of expression if they are to communicate their individual vision. Coles, I argue, has paid profound attention to the rhetorical resources of verse, and this is reflected in the unique flavour of his inimitable poetic style.

It is convenient to begin with "Photograph" from *Sometimes All Over*, a poem Coles chose to reprint twice in subsequent volumes before its appearance here. The opening lines read as follows:

> This photograph shows a man
> who is smiling
> standing beside a woman whose smile
> may in this moment be just coming
> or just going
> in a path between a cedar tree
> on their right
> and unidentifiable bushes on their left
> in bright sunlight

Coles has his eye firmly on the photographic object, which he appears to be describing in impersonal, almost clinical terms. Yet this is assuredly not mere "sliced prose," and although it may qualify as irregular verse it is certainly not "free." We notice first the careful balancing of phrases—"a man ... a woman," "just coming / or just going," "on their right ... on their left"; we may also note traces of alliteration ("smiling / standing," "bushes ... bright"), assonance ("beside ... smile," "between ... tree"), occasional regular rhyme, both internal and external ("right ... bright sunlight"), and what is sometimes described as "concept-rhyme" ("coming ... going" and "right ... left" at the ends of lines). Such effects continue throughout the poem, and several of the dominant images in the opening lines duly reappear at the end to create a formally structured close.

"Photograph" is especially significant because it raises themes and issues that are going to preoccupy Coles throughout his career. Since, after the formal opening, he reveals that the couple in the photograph are his "30-year-old unencountered / grandparents" on his mother's side, the poem represents an early instance of the subtle blending of the personal and the impersonal. Moreover, it is, by Coles' standards at this time, a relatively long poem (73 lines here), yet it contains only four sentences. The poem thus reproduces the sense of an exploratory mind in the very process of thought, piling up details and qualifications, and constantly moving ahead towards fresh insights. In addition, the poem draws attention to Coles' remarkable capacity (frequently evident in his subsequent verse) to make the simplest of words appear meaningful. The photograph recovers "a space in time" which that long-past summer would

> continue to hold open so that
> it might one day be acknowledged, as
> I would acknowledge it now, so that
> they are still there,
> or here,
> and may be encountered now

If one has not yet become accustomed to Coles' idiosyncratic style, such lines may appear loose, drifting, undisciplined—until one notices the careful placing of space-time words (there, here, now) at the end of the last three lines quoted: basic words that, by their juxtaposition, skillfully embody the emphasis on "a space in time."

The inevitable separation of parent and child is the subject of two resonantly personal poems in *Sometimes All Over*. In "For My Daughter, Now Seven Years Old", the child unthinkingly exclaims,

"'Someday I will fly away—like Peter' ... / meaning Peter Pan," and the remark elicits in the father a moving awareness of the pathos and indifference of time. It is built appropriately around the importance in childhood of repetition, implying continuity, a continuity ultimately doomed to be broken. Certain words and phrases— "Daddy," "you said," "like Peter," "space," "then," "I wonder," "you will go," "thirty years ago"—recur like the patterns in a child's kaleidoscope; again we encounter unostentatious internal rhymes—"Some day I will fly away," "flight somehow, in bed at night"—and the creative employment and placing of "now," "then," and "once" subtly reinforced by the repetitions of "time" and "space" throughout the poem.

Not all the poems are as artfully crafted as these, but the experience of writing them made other less formal but no less eloquent poems possible. "Divorced Child", for example, is more relaxed and free-flowing. A father is again thinking about a daughter, who this time has experienced a potentially traumatic severance because of the parents' divorce. Here the effectiveness depends upon the contrast between the father's sense of loss and the parallel awareness, through imagination, of the daughter's resilience and capacity to make a new start. The child is presented in the original version as

> surely happy often
>
> at most sometimes
> indirectly watchful
> of friends' unaltering homes
>
> or still, aloof a minute
> from little-kid storyhours that
> mention permanence

Here may be noted such inconspicuous yet meaningful words as "often ... sometimes," "a minute ... permanence," which attain added importance by being placed at the ends of lines. Even more effective, elsewhere in the poem, are the common but, in context, peculiarly effective adjectives (*"warm* meals," *"crisp* dresses," and in later versions from *Landslides* onwards, replacing the "unaltering homes" just quoted, first "*reliable* addresses" [my emphases]) and now "unvarying homes" in the present text. Above all, we may notice the skillful manipulation of line-breaks to draw attention to important words ("a better / new grown-up," "hands holding on / both sides," "sometimes / indirectly watchful"), a feature that characterizes all Coles' major poetry.

One more related poem, originally in *Anniversaries*, demands some brief attention here. "Sampling from a Dialogue" is another poem about the break-up of a marriage, and at a first reading it may well seem rambling and irregular. Closer inspection, however, reveals that, although the line-lengths vary drastically, and despite the violent vernacular language and rhythms ("God / damn it Marge"), the poem begins by following the traditional pattern not merely of a sonnet but of a Petrarchan sonnet, as the rhyme-scheme indicates. (We may be assisted in realizing this by the medieval references to "Roland, at Roncesvalles," and "horsemen, bright lances," where the suggestion of romance and ancient chivalry contrasts so dramatically with the modern and colloquial tone of the rest.) Yet at what should be the final line, the traditional structure collapses, and the poems spills over, "breaking the rhyme," and continues beyond the sanctioned fourteen lines. Moreover, the poem eventually ends, with one of Coles' hallmark phrases, "the catastrophe of time," on a rhyme with "rhyme" itself. "Sampling from a Dialogue" is an astonishing achievement with its ever-shifting moods and cadences, the staccato rhythms playing against the expected iambic pentameter, and the wit of the combined pun and line-break in the phrase "let's have a new / line." Only a poet who has served an intensive technical apprenticeship could have produced it.[4]

Before proceeding to some of Coles' later poems, I would like to end this section by drawing attention to another, less conspicuous feature of his style. "Photograph" is lightly punctuated, with commas and periods where necessary, but it ends without any final punctuation, as if the poem is left syntactically—and, perhaps, intellectually—open. In the case of "For My Daughter, Now Seven Years Old," the sole punctuation-marks are commas, the beginnings of sentences indicated only by capital letters. Each stanza contains three lines, all sentence-units, half of which open with the simplest of connectives: "And ..." In "Divorced Child," even the capital letters are dropped, so that, although "and" occurs three times at the beginnings of stanzas, there is no means of telling whether it indicates a new sentence or the continuation of a seemingly endless free-association interior monologue. This is a feature of many of his early poems; as a result, the narrator emerges not as a pontificating bard speaking *ex cathedra*, with the end of the poem established before the opening lines are written down, but as a sensitive, thoughtful, and often puzzled human being caught in the moment of attempting to work things out. A rapport is established between poet and reader. Coles' divided allegiances remain here in the sophisticated use of art to achieve a naturalness that seems the reverse of sophisticated, but he has succeeded in moulding a style of remarkable range and flexibility which will enable him to find the perfect medium in which to convey the more complex "transferable content" of his later work.

III

Having evolved a flexible and appropriate poetic style, Coles now found himself ready for more ambitious creative projects. It is doubtless not coincidental that the phrases "transferable content" and "usable piece of content" emerge at this point. These phrases are, as I have already suggested, open to misunderstanding, and I have perhaps performed a disservice to Coles in resurrecting them here. They help, however, to define the new emphases. Subsequently his energies are devoted to creating situations that embody and enact what he has to say and prevent the "content" from being abstracted from its essential context.

"I have a very strong feeling of preference for, if you like, the classical, I think art of any sort has to subject personal experience to certain transformations before it appears in art" (Coles in Carbert 124). This remark made in the 1994 interview provides an ideal bridge from Coles' earlier work to the more mature phase that began with *The Prinzhorn Collection*. When this book appeared in 1982, discerning readers knew that they were in the presence of an impressive and fully developed artist. Traces of the old style remain; as Susan

Glickman wrote, "'No One There' ... reincarnates the Coles of *Something All Over*" (158), though one can detect an increased impersonality even here. "Natalya Nikolayevna Goncharov" (97-8, about Pushkin's fiancée), "Three Tolstoy Poems" and "Ibsen Stanzas" which either explore and interpret the "personal" of historical figures or grapple with the relationship between artists and their art, all reach towards his ideal of "impersonality." Yet even when these poems are firmly set in the past, their tone and sentence-structure represent a determination on Coles' part to catch the rhythms of late twentieth-century speech—educated speech, to be sure, but still contemporary. The past invariably becomes a subject for meditation in the present.

"The Prinzhorn Collection" itself, the poem that gives its name to the volume in which it first appeared, is a significant development in Coles' art. The most obvious and substantial product of his European "wander-years," it is unusual for Coles in being, albeit obliquely, a politically committed poem. It is also remarkable, like its successors *K. in Love* and *Little Bird*, for its use of the letter as a literary form. Letters may be regarded as equivalents in the world of writing to photographs in the world of pictorial art. Like photographs, they isolate a particular moment in time, yet can survive within time to be re-read and re-experienced under totally different conditions. They are objects that have come down to us from the past, are fixed in time, yet preserve an illusion of fluidity and immediacy; in many instances, though intensely personal documents, they even qualify as works of art themselves.

Here Coles produces a complicated "Chinese box" effect. The actual objects making up the collection (authentic, historical documents, as a note explains, exhibited at a Munich art-gallery) are filtered to us through an unnamed German curator/narrator from Dr. Prinzhorn, the medical director of an asylum (who took the trouble to preserve them, perhaps as an anti-Fascist gesture); Prinzhorn in turn inherited the collection from a possibly mad—or sick—predecessor who hoarded the materials inhumanely and from dubious psychological motives. These objects are described by the curator in a fabricated verse-letter written in a conspicuously self-conscious English. They consist of "drawings, letters and / Journals by the inmates of a nineteenth century / *Irrenanstalt* (madhouse)," psychological documents transformed into art by the very act of displaying them in a public gallery. Most of the drawings illustrate sexual fantasies or, more likely, abuses, with implications for the political situation of their time; dating from the Bismarck years, they were preserved secretly during the Nazi era when they would have been stigmatized as *Entartate Kunst* or decadent art, and are now displayed in a late-twentieth-century ambience of arguable maturity. All this is significant in itself; even more interesting are the letters (the only part of the collection, obviously, that can be reproduced within the poem), including those of one inmate, Joseph Grebing, who writes to his father in a desperate but vain attempt to procure his release. These are, then, letters quoted within a letter; moreover (since they were never delivered but docketed instead in the director's files), they are written into an echoless void, which, for all the curator knows, may be the fate of his own letter. Yet ironically, *because* they were never delivered, Grebing's letters have been preserved in art. The curator's private missive, of course, is imagined to be preserved in the same way, within Coles' art.

The image of the madhouse, and confinement within a madhouse, has profound political and artistic implications. "An entire human-condition is here," we are told, conveyed in eloquent messages "from / the borders of despair." The poem is contained within its own claustrophobic form, its meaning imprisoned within the curator's letter just as the inmates are imprisoned within the asylum. Commentators have, perhaps significantly, interpreted the curator/narrator in different ways, some stressing his "sympathy" (Fagan 22), others his "fascination with the sexually perverse" (Djwa and Hatch 347). Glickman is more cautious—and, I suspect, closer to the mark—in emphasizing the way in which he is unwillingly "driven into 'amateur metaphysics' by the implications of what he has seen" (167). I would suggest that Coles, who is once more struggling with his own dichotomies, deliberately creates a situation in which the acutely personal (Grebing's *cri de coeur*) is doubly transformed—or hijacked—into impersonal art, once by the organization of the art exhibition, once by Coles himself. The curator is forced to address the personal when, as Glickman notes (167), he would prefer to "confine his responses to his 'competency, the visible.'" He is as puzzled—and as troubled—as we are; just as he struggles to interpret the documents he is displaying, so we have to interpret the nuances of the meanings expressed in what is for him a foreign language. And Coles, with amazing skill and an even more amazing economy, succeeds in creating for him an individual style or idiolect which is totally distinct from his own. He draws here upon all the rhetorical devices I have examined in the earlier poems (except rhyme), but they are absorbed into a seamless language that fits the curator perfectly and is like nothing else that Coles has written, before or since.

If we omit *Landslides* (1986), most of which consisted of previously published poems, Coles' next two books, *K. in Love* (1987) and *Little Bird* (1991), both offer themselves as letters, though both use the epistolary form as little more than a springboard for more elaborate literary constructs. Ostensibly, according to the "Note" at the back of the original edition but not reproduced here, *K. in Love* consists of a series of "poem-letters" that "owe their coming-into-being to a concentrated several weeks' reading of the letters and journals of Franz Kafka." But this is a little deceptive. Coles has since revealed (one is tempted to write "confessed"!) that they derive in the main from "notes that I'd been making to myself over a number of years" (Carbert 125), about half of them written before he encountered Kafka's love-letters.[5]

From the literary-critical viewpoint, this explanation enables us to locate the volume at the very centre of Coles' preoccupations. First, it is germane to his attempt to make his poetry "welcoming" to readers who don't habitually read verse. He sees the poems as "a series of very, I think, accessible little lyrics," and insists that, despite the Kafka frame, the book as a whole, in excluding "any intellectual academic references," is "as simple and transparent" as he could make it (Carbert 125, 126). Moreover, though Coles claims in the "Note," somewhat ingenuously, that, while he was composing the poem-letters, "the personality ... of their narrator-writer moved gradually further and further away from me, closer to Kafka," the reverse may in fact be nearer the truth. One suspects, indeed, that the "intense, gentle, ... remarkably nice man" who "almost shows through here" is a happy amalgam of the best aspects of both Kafka and Coles.[6] What has happened is that Coles is once again moving away from the "personal" by placing his own love-lyrics at a temporal and spatial remove in the mouth of a fellow-artist and presented as if they existed as distanced historical documents.

Little Bird purports to be a verse-letter ("this interminable letter" written by Coles to his father after the latter's death. Tonally, it could not be further removed from *K. in Love*, yet an intriguing possible connection exists: while reading Kafka, Coles almost certainly encountered a prose-letter written by Kafka to his still-living father (this has been published separately as *Letter to His Father*), in which he offers his own firm and devastating account of their unhappy relationship. The parallels are considerable. In both cases, the clash involves the age-old generation-gap between materialist father and artistically minded son. Each writer tended to flaunt his literary and "Bohemian" interests in the face of his practical, no-nonsense, non-literary progenitor, and each attempts to make peace while simultaneously producing an unrepentant *apologia pro vita sua*. Otherwise, however, the works are radically different. Kafka offers a desperate justification of his position in clearly-argued prose that poignantly conveys the uncomfortable realities of lived life. Coles at first appears to be doing the same thing, yet, because his response takes the form of an extended poem—274 four-line stanzas in the present version—and because the argument turns on language (and silence), the result is a stylistic *tour de force* full of exhilarating shifts of tone and reference, a triumph of rhetorical and poetic wit that ultimately takes precedence over the biographical nature of the subject-matter.

Yet although the poetic style is a dramatic departure for Coles, other aspects of *Little Bird* are decidedly familiar. Again we are confronted with a parent-child relationship. Moreover, the relentless passing of time accounts for the poem's very existence, since it is offered as a substitute for the "longed-for / heart-to-heart" that never took place in the father's lifetime. The poem is an attempt, belatedly, to "build some kind / of bridge towards you", but the father's death constitutes an inexorable boundary between "then" and "now," words that once again recur continually.

A crucial moment in the postulated dialogue between son and father occurs when Coles asserts, "*Making us / whole, father, is what /*

all this seems to be about," and immediately imagines the father's probably gruff and deflating reply, "Sounds very grand." This creates a climax at what is, in fact, the central core of the poem. Earlier, we are told that the father "took little pleasure in such / [verbal] flamboyancies, and not overmuch / in language either," and this aggravates the son's romantic yearning towards the world of poetry and art. Yet the poem's colloquial, even slangy style itself eschews "flamboyancies," and this signals the extent to which he is prepared to move towards the father. Looking back, he recognizes his earlier verbal pyrotechnics as "ornate stuff," "antic stuff.". He is even able to acknowledge his young self as "an anointed / asshole." Poets and artists eventually become "that babbling tribe / I joined so early / and love so little now."

The astonishing stylistic fact about *Little Bird* is that the poem which began with an ornate and literary formality—"You will not need / Achilles' ghost, / nor Aeneas'; nor greet / others from that host ..." (175)—can also contain lines like the following: "... well, like I say, / when it works it's great / but so often there's just / no way, / know what I mean?" This is possibly the greatest concentration of cliché— deliberate cliché, of course—ever assembled in a verse! Yet there is as much technical poetic skill displayed in the latter passage as in the former. The poem, while ostentatiously trying to establish some imagined rapport with the father, is actually a triumphant justification of the anointed asshole's determination to be a poet. Like all Coles' work, it is finely crafted, but nowhere else are the traditional features of poetry (rhyme, quatrains, etc.) so boldly combined with vernacular, slang, fashionable discontinuities—and, above all, Coles' characteristic extended sentences, revived from his earlier style, that suggest so artfully the rambling prolixities of ordinary speech. The poem that reproduces the uneasy relationship with the father's "then" becomes a vivid evocation of the son's and poet's "now."

Coles was himself puzzled by *Little Bird*. When, in this context, Fagan mentioned Coles' strictures concerning "confessional poetry," the poet admitted that "*Little Bird* ... goes against what I have most begun to feel that I wanted poetry to be about" (22). I would argue, however, that the poem is saved from confessional excess by its (for Coles) unusually conspicuous artifice. In the Carbert interview he recalled how the "mechanical need to find a rhyme" led *away* from the personal or self-indulgent (126). The content is indeed "transferable"—because father-son hostilities are common, the poem, as Coles remarked, "can mean something to persons other than one's cousins or one's aunts" (Carbert 126)—but, thanks to the stylistic pyrotechnics and the fascination of the rhymes, both Don Coles and Jack Coles have become transformed or, we might say, unpersonalized, into created larger-than-life figures within a vast and absorbing human drama.

IV

Coles' last two volumes, *Forests of the Mediaeval World* (1993) and *Kurgan* (2000) develop even further the artistry and poise developed in the earlier poems reproduced in the present collection. They return to the shorter forms, and many of the themes, of his earlier work, yet move forward to a greater complexity and resonance. The two name-poems are cases in point. Both are medium-length (three pages), yet the ramifications and implications are at least as great as those of "The Prinzhorn Collection." In "Forests of the Mediaeval World," a modern love-story is played out against the image of the vast forests of medieval Europe, and the fact that the forests have now dwindled, or in some cases vanished, throws an ominous and poignant shadow over the human relationship in the present. In "Kurgan No.10," a contemporary archaeologist digs up the grave of a two-thousand-year-old princess, and his responses ring new and brilliant changes on Coles' fascination with "then" and "now" and the intricacies of the "personal" and the "impersonal." Reading them and many of the other poems in the same volumes, I am reminded of a shrewd comment on the art of Mavis Gallant to the effect that her short stories contain more substance than the full-length novels of most other writers.

In addition to eighteen dazzling new poems, *Kurgan* contains fifteen reprints of previously published material. Many of these have been quietly but subtly revised, and this brings me conveniently to the last point that needs to be made here. Coles is notorious among Canadian poets for continually tinkering with his poems. In the

Carbert interview, he remarked: "As for rewriting, I rewrite and rewrite. I guess I enjoy that more than anything." Much of this process occurs, of course, before the poem in question appears in print for the first time, but in Coles' case it can also occur whenever he has the chance to reprint. Thus it is not uncommon for a Coles poem to exist in three–sometimes, even four or five–slightly different versions. The publication of this new selection has given him yet another opportunity to substitute certain words for others and (especially) to alter the position of his line-breaks. Because he is a highly skilled tinkerer, the changes are invariably improvements, and a good many of the earlier poems are therefore more polished and effective in the versions printed here. He has also chosen to omit poems that no longer satisfy him (only 27 of the 49 poems in *Sometimes All Over* are preserved here) and to shorten others (*Little Bird* is reduced by 22 stanzas and many others are radically revised). All this is Coles' privilege, and it enables him to offer this book as constituting, with the two later volumes, the summation of his art. Apprentice poets (and specialist scholars) will need to compare these texts with earlier ones, and such research can prove fascinating for anyone interested in the evolution of poetic mastery. For most readers, however, it is enough that the following pages represent the best earlier works of one of the most accomplished poets of our time—in Canada or elsewhere.

W. J. Keith

This introduction is a revised version of the earlier sections of an article, "A Preference for the Classical: Notes on the Art of Don Coles," first published in *Canadian Poetry* 48 (Spring/Summer 2001), 13-37.)

1. I have noticed only one clear verbal echo of Eliot in Coles' poetry: the appositional phrase "linger in / those chambers" in the late "Hector Alone" (from *Kurgan*), an obvious allusion to the close of "The Love Song of J. Alfred Prufrock."

2. This, too, may represent a covert, perhaps even unconscious debt to Eliot's modernism, also well known for its "impersonality."

3. In the present critical climate, it is perhaps necessary to point out that I am aware that the poet and the "I" of the poem need not be identical, and are often separate. In this poem, however, and in a number of others discussed in the course of this introduction, the distinction does not apply.

4. It is probably a significant indication of the decline in the skills of close reading that, when I set this poem for commentary in a senior undergraduate class several years ago, no student noticed the Petrarchan substructure.

5. The diligent researcher will therefore find little of use in either Kafka's *Letters to Felice* (Felice Bauer) or the *Letters to Milena* (Milena Jesenská). At best, some of Coles' lyrics represent a distillation of some of Kafka's tone, attitudes, and somewhat quirky though endearing fantasies. The more troublesome qualities in Kafka's actual letters—his self-conscious references to his Jewish ancestry, his interminable complaints about not receiving letters and the vagaries of the postal service, and his general sense of anguish and desperation—are all absent.

6. In particular, one curious detail—perhaps the only "intellectual academic" reference in the sequence—bears out this conclusion, and may even be intended to do so. In one poem, the narrator quotes several lines from Edward Thomas's poem "The Owl" (166). It is not absolutely impossible that Kafka had ever encountered this poem, but it is highly improbable. Yet Thomas belongs in the "Hardy-Larkin line," and is just the kind of poet likely to appeal to Coles himself, who is surely the speaker here.

WORKS CITED IN INTRODUCTION

Carbert, Michael. "Don Coles. No Safer Place: An Interview." *Quarry* 43:1 (1994), 117-29.

Coles, Don. "The Hardy-Larkin Line." Rev. of Christopher Wiseman, *The Upper Hand*. *Canadian Forum* 62 (June-July 1982), 36.

Djwa, Sandra, and Ronald Hatch. "Poetry," in "Letters in Canada 1982," *University of Toronto Quarterly* 52 (Summer 1983), 343-58.

Fagan, Cary. "Mutability and Meditation." *Books in Canada* 21:1 (February 1992), 22-4.

Glickman, Susan. "All in War with Time: the Poetry of Don Coles." *Essays on Canadian Writing* 35 (Winter 1987), 156-70.

Leavis, F. R. *The Living Principle: 'English' as a Discipline of Thought*. London: Chatto & Windus, 1975.

Macmillan of Canada. "Trade News." Press-release advertising *The Prinzhorn Collection*, 1982.

SOMETIMES ALL OVER (1975)

HOW WE ALL SWIFTLY

My God how we all swiftly, swiftly
unwrap our lives, running from
one rummaged secret to the next
like children among their birthday stuff—
a shout, a half-heard gasp here
and for a while bliss somewhere else
when the one thing we asked for all year
is really there and practically as perfect
as we knew it would be. Those beckoning passes
into what's ahead: first words, the run
without a fall, a bike, those books,
a girl whose nakedness is endless in our bed,
and a few public stunts with results that
partly please us. And on we go, my God how
restlessly among glimpsed profiles turning and
undarkening towards us as we reach them—lucky
the ones who will more than briefly enter
that intricate journey which while it shines proves
some of the children right.

BUSY AT NIGHT AT SOME ADULT THING

busy at night at some adult thing
like walking about my house
or sitting with mingled thoughts

an indistinct sound from outside can remind me
of being in bed some early summer evening
when I was nine or ten

and hearing through my bedroom window
noises from streets
where people were still up

like an unemphatic calling out
on the next block, or some
not necessarily near footsteps on a sidewalk

or small and veering cries that meant
older children were still outside playing

sounds rising out of the streets

I did not envy any of that
it was a feeling of the world going on
in a composed distance

meant only to be listened to

I was not anxious about it
I think I knew it was a time for other people
to be doing those things

I think I understood that soon
I would be down there too

they are still there
those unentered summer evenings
and those small veering cries and footsteps
and callings-out

they are still an intact net of sound
spread out below that bedroom window
promising endless things

CHILD'S SANDCASTLE

Beside the castle slowly
subsiding in the sand
the giantess drowses

In surrounding vistas of sand
her pail and shovel drift

In the advancing afternoon
behind their tiny stone windows
hidden lords and ladies move
anxiously among their rich
morning lives

DEATH OF WOMEN

Everywhere they were just
wiped out. Supermarkets
hauled them away in shopping carts,
libraries and kindergartens closed
with unreassuring bulletins,
for as long as it lasted
husbands, waking, found them staring
at ceilings or sprawled in doorways
to the children's room, as if
it was there they had felt they must
explain hardest. Anthropologists
and all-night launderette manageresses,
a naked blackhaired princess
in a rocksinger's *Mitteleuropa* hunting lodge,
their faces unpredictably hinting
astonishing peace or war
in appointments of love and birth
and the gestures of the day—
they all went.
By the third day it was over.
Statistics were assembled, it was agreed
the world was altered.
Life began on the adjusted basis.

Then new women appeared.

DIVORCED CHILD

away from those bad voices now

and safe among
warm meals broadloom a good school and
small crisp dresses

a better
new grown-up with her,
matinees and restaurant-tables
still for three

and for crossing streets
hands holding on
both sides

surely happy often

at most sometimes
indirectly watchful
of friends' unvarying homes

or still, aloof a minute
from little-kid storyhours
that mention permanence

but not by any stretch
of the emotions
to be characterized by
a word like grief

and for sure not thinking, right now, about

the fleet of plasticine Chinese junks
sailing
across the floor of this upstairs cottage bedroom
I guess since the end of last summer

"DON'T MARRY, PIERRE, YOU'LL WASTE YOUR LIFE IN TRIVIALITIES"

Somewhere between peace
and war, Tolstoy as Prince André Bolkonsky
counsels a half-disbelieving other self—

Bézuhkov, leaned forward, listens,
the lenses of his gold-framed specs
reflecting a best friend's wisdom.

Ah, his whole future hovers!

He foresees those thousand scenes,
nights staring at his desk, she's somewhere,
his mind's work's baffled and postponed—

impasses his body often resolves but
like obdurate fate will re-encounter again
and again.

Anxious to free his spirit from all this
he'll walk around, stand a lot in streets
and parks and squares, glance at notebooks
and pictures and passing faces

consider in silence his surroundings, alert
for intrusions of meaning, of unrealized
ambitions and unrealistic hopes for goodness

Out from a dream he can never control
grows a glowing core of light, it is always
an unknown kneeling woman

opening her naked arms.

DRIVING AT AN EASY SIXTY

Driving at an easy sixty along
this early-morning empty highway,
sunlight growing on fields to
either side of me, unasked out of
the approaching and then receding
barns and woods and hills there gathers
a glimpsed reflection of myself
30 or 40 years either side of now.

Infant and old man, each was or will be
a stage of stopped landscapes where
one prospect was all I had or will have,
each of them as sure on either side
of this capable hour as sunlight on the fields.
Briefly, now, I drive between them,
harvesting countrysides between charmed
and foolproof moorings.

Resting once after play you looked at me and said, "Daddy",
    and "Daddy" until I had time
and you said, "Someday I will fly away—like Peter", and
    again, "like Peter", you said
meaning Peter Pan, the story we had read

And I don't suppose you noticed what happened next but
time hollowed a space around me then, your words moved in
    that space
I could have wept, probably did not but then I don't weep
    enough generally

Since then it's two years and I think of it often, the space
follows me, your voice still a five-year-old's, the clear
    statement
never intended to hurt or be remembered

And I fearful of reminding you, nothing and nobody could
    force a repetition
nevertheless remembering, a prophecy from resting time
words spoken into a space I must once have had too

And I wonder when you will go, perhaps you are quietly
preparing flight somehow, in bed at night growing peacefully
    towards it, and I wonder
what words did I put into that space thirty years ago

I wonder if you will go
I wonder if the space simply was there and you felt it and
    knew what it was asking
I wonder if I am doing whatever I said thirty years ago to
    whoever was listening

FOUR MEDITATIONS AFTER THE EVENT

I

Which of us would have believed it but
even retreating ranges of sad and happy still
show up even though you don't. You won't
have lost sight of them either, is my guess.
Way off there whole countrysides light up,
high ledges pour colour—then all these
fade off, clouds intervene. Whatever
the metaphor, things alter. Which is
all right, alteration I mean, a help
when it happens. *If* it happens. Meanwhile I
riffle trusted poets' pages, hoping to find one that
still works.

II

I have no continual face for you now
and your best words don't seem to be
making it over the just plain weird
terrain we ended up on, although who says
any conclusions have to be drawn from
that? But what about these things still
floating off my skin whenever I'm
alone with it, sense of a mouth lifting or
a look from you so prescient in its timing
(arrival and departure) that I didn't merely
love it, I practically *trusted* it. Also sometimes
when there's no mirror around I can see
your smile on my face.

III

There used to be so much specialness
around (kindnesses neither of us knew
we had in us, small comments that came
when they would help most and left off
ditto, or, you know what I'll say next,
your body everywhere so wonderful, me
its detailed corroborator) that of course
nobody else was half as interesting as he
used to be. Or she. Only sometimes
things like this would brim over and
whoever'd been with us might, when
they left, find themselves heading off
into a better kind of night. Better
than the one they'd come in from, I mean.

IV

I would like to know what it means that
our really good times aren't the ones
I remember best. It's as if I was never sure
we could go on being like that and so
didn't want to study it, or us, in case
there'd been some mistake which a close scrutiny
would only make obvious. Now it's those
character analyses you left me with
that I find myself examining, even though
I'm still not sure whether last lines like those
come from a really prophetic place
or are just amazed sounds out of
the unspecific extreme repertoire, that I can
test myself against.

GIRL READING F. SCOTT FITZGERALD
ON THE SUBWAY

Although as a rule he regards his life as
a random arrangement, a style he enjoys,
attentive only in hours when a poem's
unproven gathering noise

shifts in its pre-language place,
many's the time he'd agree that his thoughts
(blurred by seasons and riding around)
don't seem to bring home the brilliant plots

he made for himself in a former year;
makes do instead with a furtive ache
for this or that, the odd safe dream
that a finally welcoming day will break.

But across the aisle her gentle knees
supporting *Tender is the Night*
annul all this, profoundly he sees
that Fitzgerald's bright

and fervent snows move her
as always him, the little breathless
runs at love while years and talent blur—
he flickers with a luminous guess:

all he's done well or ill is merging here
and all his roads were right,
now, as old journeys clear,
now, while two lives sway near...

Not counting a few higher dramas although
aware, yes, of exiled heroines and
absorpt times, this now is briefer air he's
gathering and quicker faces, sifting for news
of self and other altering humankind from
years before he'd learned how every soon-lost
sight will last. Finds those in evening towns
who turned and smiled and those who stayed
a while, or not, clear words or none at all—
they arrive and pose in their by-now familiar
way, somehow they knew what's perfect, then
they go. Is sure they must have blurred those
silhouettes as carelessly as he, walked on
and never guessed how they're marooned
in scenes they dare not leave or add to, how
here their motions cease—pausing in dark time
like bright haiku showing him
his unexplained ecstatic life.

IT IS A MORE THAN COMMON PRIVILEGE

It is a more than common privilege
to be allowed to enter
your body

which is so unarguably
whiter and softer and better arranged
than mine

Each entering is a passage
towards new stations
of intimate plenitude

(and more)

My mind rocks with
your naked rocking body
so lightly balancing

enters into it,
uncommanded lifts
past me

rises to a place not mine
which calmly greets this
more than common privilege

as its right.

He wonders, lifting them from their attic box, how
will he justify his time away,
him with his funny runs after a life, about ready now
to grant they had a point choosing to stay.
Stands them up, the cold
of plenty of years up here coating these old
quickdraws since that casual hour
that ended play—
and easily, unsurprised to find themselves
standing again, they restore simple plots,
old solved adventures, himself up here
in vast time.
Their flaking rudimentary faces ambush
his eyes, he sees they'll approve
all this only if he can show
he's happier—no, more settled, more
certain, yes, more steadfast now—
has been in places where he's learned these things,
his years below.

MOVING DAY

for Sarah

afternoon's almost over in the emptying house and
the van's an hour gone, only sleeping-bags on the floor
for tonight and minor detritus for tomorrow's early exit

hints of years-suppressed echoes gathering already
as my wife and I shift baskets of loose sounds
through widening rooms to the front hall

passing the back bedroom window with an armful of holy
junk I see our daughter on the slatted bench in the yard
under a heavy-leafed tree with the neighbour's girl
out there, her number one buddy, and am about to
call something at them, not necessarily
an order but for sure an intrusion

then the way they're sitting, the angle
of their thin T-shirted shoulders against the white horizontal
of fence at the property line, the murmur
of their voices

stops me

and I stand, presager of nothing
but remembering I've seen those kids out there
at least an hour ago

a long time for two generally-running
nine-year-olds to stay put in one place

and it occurs to me to eavesdrop but
even with the window open I can't hear them,
only can see them sitting there, and a nod now
from the neighbour's darkhaired kid and
a silence and then a voice again, and their faces
turn to look at maybe the slats of bench between them,
two white motions reminding me about
late and darkening

so again I almost call to them, thinking of time
but all at once that's out

and I lean against the windowframe realizing it's likely
their last talk and although there is no telling
how good their words are
the yard's flowing with a lot of stages of growing-up
that from now on they're each going to go through
separately among their own sights and sounds

and although it's obvious they can't consciously have been
trying to remedy or even absorb that,
you have to admit they are posed as if there's some kind of
very big and unfamiliarly coloured guess
ballooning out there

and their heads move to look apparently in directions like
the fence, the heavy leaves, their two houses,
games and hours they've played and games and hours
they may be agreeing not to play

and seeming so calm and intent about it that
I don't know why else they're still sitting there
talking so quietly nobody can hear them
unless it's because they almost know
that an afternoon isn't too long to spend securing
a time that's safe enough for two nine-year-olds to enter and
always run together in

MY GRANDFATHER, MY GRANDMOTHER

Alone this morning here
in this cottage where you lived
the careful last summers of your contracting lives,
rows of rain falling from the eaves,
the rainbarrel irrelevantly filling
and the disabled wooden sawhorse
upended years now
among the water-heavy trees,
the dark furnishings of this room refreshed
by a more colourful generation
and approximately new prints and fabrics
on walls and windows,
even the slow-arrived shadows of
wall-ranked copper saucepans
noticeably nowhere,
the rooms receding from you
each year and not much, I guess, that would be
easily familiar,
I would like you to know,
if this can be a way,
that now in a stubborn season
behind my eyes
those quiet secure summers
still go on,
days still begin early and end
unannounced at sundown,
rows of rain fall from the eaves,
the rainbarrel brims and is
reported upon,
the sawhorse retains its upright purpose,
these images return
out of the years, they are all
ordinary but of some account,
this place is yours,
you are here.

Seeing a boy and girl hand in hand
along this evening street
doesn't impair my present hour—
what acts and words will follow them here
have been or may be mine, or so, at least,
the familiar human distance they leave me for
will let me think.

But Osip Mandelstam's lines to his woman,
"We shall meet in Petersburg as though we had
buried the sun there"—with seams of
deep, unauthorized light
sunder my unused life.

PHOTOGRAPH

This photograph shows a man
who is smiling
standing beside a woman whose smile
may in this moment be just coming
or just going
in a path between a cedar tree
on their right
and unidentifiable bushes on their left
in bright sunlight.
She is wearing a wide white hat
and a loose dress,
he a dark suit, white shirt
with stiff collar,
and a tie with a large knot—
costumes which, since it is evidently
a hot day in summer,
indicate the picture is not recent.
I'm moved to know that in fact
this summer is seventy years ago
and the man and woman
so seemingly at ease here
are my 30-year-old unencountered
grandparents, who died
three years after this photograph
was taken (as we, outside
the photograph, know, but inside it
they do not: my mother is perhaps
almost inside the photograph,
perhaps just beyond it,
perhaps lying in the shade
of the cedar to their right,
and will soon be one year old)
and to know, too, that my mother
will live her life among persons
not present in this photograph

and so will never adequately
be told of these smiles, this
afternoon of sunlight on a path
(how, partly shadowed
under the wide white hat,
her mother's eyes moved to
the sounds around them, the cicada
in the high trees, how
the warmth of the afternoon lay
across her father's shoulders
on the dark cloth), the hot green smell
of cedar moving in their minds.
It reminds me of Villon and other
unrecovered seasons, but better than
these it focuses for me a minute when
hopeful, unprophetic things fused with
two people who smiled just then to
invincibly form a place in time which
(as perhaps in that minute they knew,
and so entered it with great anxiety,
but also with great love) that summer
would not carelessly release
but would continue to hold open so that
it might one day be acknowledged, as
I would acknowledge it now, so that
they are still there,
or here,
and may be encountered now
if I can make the afternoon
absolute enough, the smell of cedar
endless enough and green
in its summer heat, if I can make
their smiles turn towards her,
standing, now, and older,
and facing them
in the path between the bushes and the cedar
in the bright sunlight
smiling

PHOTOGRAPH IN A STOCKHOLM NEWSPAPER FOR MARCH 13, 1910

Here is a family so little famous their names
are not recorded. They stand, indistinct
as though they know it's right, in this slum
courtyard in weak sunlight. The darksuited
father's hand rests on his small son's shoulder,
mother and daughter are on either side of
the open door. It is a Sunday or we may be sure
they would not be together like this, motionless
for the photographer's early art.

To be moved by these people must seem sentimental.
We're here years too late to hope their blurred
faces will unpack into features we can side with or
against, or expect these bodies will release themselves
into those next shapes on which we'll base a plot.

But that's it: not here they are, but there they
were. Safe now from even their own complexities—
what luck not to be asked their names!—and proof
against our most intricate pursuit, they stand in
a blur that seems no error of focus but an inspired
rendering of how they chose to last, admitting
nothing except that once they were there. That hand
rested on that shoulder. The four of them stood
there. The door was left open. There was
some weak sunlight.

We shall never learn more. They seem miraculous.
They persuade me all may be well.

if healthy and in midst of my years
watching these high trees sway
in moderate evening wind
I can glimpse through grey revolving branches
such absolutely alien distances,
what of the unanchored roaming senses of
my friend whose once so fair and generous mind
is now marooned in a small bedroom,
his only place of intermittent safety?

when my world thins will I
veer and wheel in wind, or see
through sundering branches
an endurable sky

SYLVIA (1932-1963)

Of course I don't know. Only sometimes
we can make a decent guess, places
others go we've never been to, a kind of
closeness seems possible. How it would be
if we ever went there. And my guess is
you pretty well knew this could be a healing,
or the final form of the nightmare, something
entire was near. Sounds about to become
words, the fractured unresolved shapes of
a life, islands joining up—a long-shot,
unpredictable event consciously sensing its
chance, not quite random motions gathering
and filling the room, chattering just outside or
for some of those hours, my guess goes on to say,
half-inside your lamp's circled light. The two
small ones left with a neighbour—"wait here
until I come". Then back to this, hardly bearable
excitement of the appointment, images arriving
from recent corners of the room, the abandoned and
suddenly perhaps revelatory marriage, ocean-distant
childhood—imagine beginning to hear even
the long-travelling sounds from a finally audible
infancy! That totally glimpsed country, long
coastline most of us don't get to see. What it's all
about, we're not trained for. Too easy to say
this killed you, naturally there were other matters,
close-up sadnesses we can understand, love
gone. Nevertheless that's survivable, look at us,
proofs everywhere. But all of it, the rushing
unpostponable clarity of first-and-last words
onto the page, unmanageable form of father,
early warm waters and talent like an unassisted
pending birth now smileless and sober darkly

looming through thirty-one years of intermittently
diagnosed signals. Into sight now and undismissably
here, this last deep self, self who, the evidence is,
can only leave. We are still here, safe in the neighbourhood,
like waiting children.

THE HOUSE

Thirty years now since he lived here,
former neighbours gone of course, no one
to recognize him or from across the street call
an easy day's greeting (so easy once why
couldn't a sound or two, unattended-to then,
have hung back for a better day?)—
they're all part of it but are not why he comes.
It's the house, that same closed door guarding
his first ten years. Stops always across the road,
in imagination opens that door, steps
small inside and like a youngest son in
dragon country mounts the dark-grained
staircase, perilously across the carpet past
his parents' room, enters his own. Shadows
and wallpaper with rosy clouds, his bed,
a window opening down to the early-morning
yard; downstairs the blue soft chair, closet
for scarves and mitts, its smell of varnish
invading and sweeping him steeply back
towards scenes he thinks he'll fall towards
if he keeps going. Old daydreams
move here, reviving deep air, and
early-morning voices from rooms around
shake him with sudden dread and love.
These sights and sounds restore to him
fearsome but also familiar (enthralling, edgeless,
limitless) thoughts he again believes he will
someday enter and understand, easily his taller self
will see into that lucid space he knows the grownups
live in…none of this will happen. None. But
here they are like dams of time, pent to burst back
through all his years away, all over now
if he goes in.

THE WAY SHE LOOKS AT ME

her look which says I know you will
astonish me

which says
my delight forms uncontrollable to receive
your mind's gift

surely I'm not the only one who sees
this sweet space binding us...

THINKING OF YOU TONIGHT

Thinking of you tonight
who do not love me,

I provisionally write
who loves me
who loves me.

Such surge of power!
Your private face lifts,

daybreaks seem,
such a look, O

continents beckon, pages
cry out—...

Such purposeless act,
I lie against life—

I would much rather lie
against you. But

tomorrow when I ask
it may come in handy.

It may surround with a brief nonplussedness
your straightforward *No.*

TO AN OLDER BROTHER BORN DEAD

I'd never pretend that knowing about you
has been, you know, really and permanently
bad, because the other kids were usually
around and I never much minded being shown
the family photos that ignored you. Still,
I know I could have used you a few times,
even a postcard from wherever you might
have been could have saved me a couple of
my dumber moves. Or, who knows, our talks
walking together those summer evenings when
because I'd learned never to expect you
I went out without waiting—not to exaggerate,
but anything all shifts the mosaic, doesn't it,
so those could have been enough. Somewhere
in there you'd have found the time. Though
the fact is I imagine you mostly listening,
you'll probably understand why: and pardoning
like a wise young monk, and smiling, and with
unused eyes. Even more, though—since
if you had shown up in those old photos
everyone else would have had to move—
I think of you living *my* life but always
that one year ahead: uncrowded because
how can I know who else to put there,
who else to see, but noticing the world and
happy because you can remember feeling
forty years ago that it was fading before you'd
even reach it. Oh, you could have spent
the entire time away but at least you'd
have been somewhere, instead of like this
where you've been nowhere or, for all
I know, where you've been thinking you were
the lucky one all along. You'd be surprised
how much I'd have trusted you.

WHITE HORSES OF THE SPANISH
RIDING SCHOOL IN VIENNA

As our guidebook says, these white horses are
legendary. From our marbled balcony beside
the crystal chandliers which light them, we watch
the fulfilling below us of the intricate patterns
of the Lippizaner generations—the packed haunch's
practiced tremor, the raised hoof's slow descent
through a solved space, glistenings of minute motions
suppressed in extra air. The gifted's extra time.
The scarlet captains cantering to the pleasure
of dead Emperors. This dirt floor muffles sound,
we almost understand how they can have circled
and crossed, mingled and emerged in line again
through so many of our inattentive far-off afternoons.
But I look down and strain to catch any secret gesture
towards my life, to sense a slender turning that might
admit them. Here in this unexpected palace they move
into my mind along passages normally patrolled
by images hardly ever so graceful or disciplined,
decades of adult life almost never free from doubt,
detoured journeys towards how many half-glimpsed
clearings, hours of subterfuge like this to save a child's
smile even one more afternoon. The white horses
flow discreetly among these, naturally there are no
collisions.

YOUR BODY BEFORE WINTER

Leaving you any of these mornings is how
I learn the world's benign.
Walking in it I do not disturb anything.

Buying the paper has never been as easy as now,
some of the clusters of faces I see practically shine,
and even congested and rainy sidewalks allow

my slippery speed as never before.
It's obvious I keep finding the hour for
entering each day that most suits its style—

or a level, some passage, its anxieties never find,
a corridor of a special helpful kind.
Though other times I think it's merely that for that while

nobody sees me. Getting up and leaving you
naked in bed is such an act against gravity
my packed eyes are private all day,

I'm richly absent from these runs away.
Leaving, I'm still deep in that white weather you save
for me, deeper than any weather that's round about—

I'd never be safe again if I really left you,
or let the rain, or anything, wash me out.

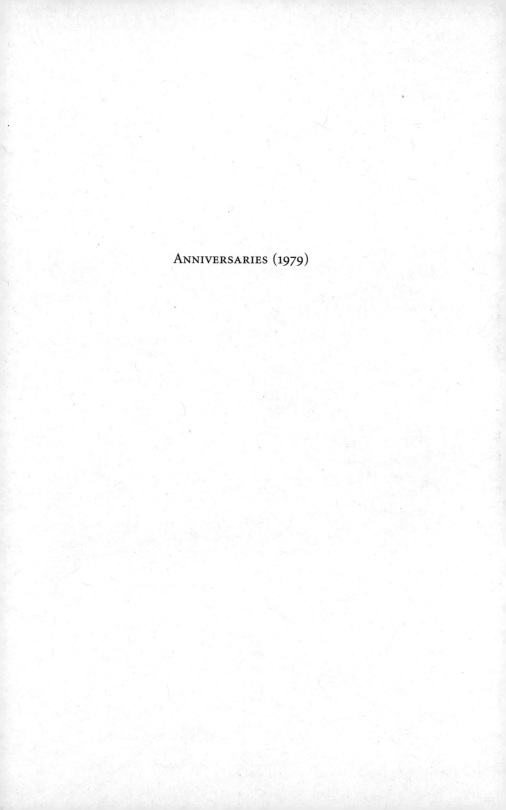

Anniversaries (1979)

OLD

Unspoken conversations with my mother in a 'chronic'
(= helpless + dying) ward

1

Hint of a body under thick blankets
beneath these white tubes of light,
stranded among a dozen lolling
heads, the occasional indiscreet veined leg,
and the donated tely blinking—

this is not what you imagined.

2

What's happening to you, curled
months under these rampaging bedclothes?
One day I'll find they have
overpowered you. But today
you open your eyes in an accomplished way.

3

Some who can more or less walk
pause at doorways, contemplate, unreliably
pajama'd, a probable fate. Call for Nursie,
for a moistening of lips. Sniff, vestigially
accountable, the air for trouble.

4

Jeremy Taylor felt certain of
the great tables of His mercy.
From puffy skin, white sheets,
your eyes blue as cornflowers
are wittily skeptical.

5

I fantasize you sitting up in a minute
in full possession again.
What a word-hoard spilling from
almost a year's absolute reticence!
But you decide against it.

6

"I should be a star in Heaven"
Wittgenstein wrote in a letter,
"But here I am stuck on earth."
I quote his complaint to you conspiratorially,
Adding to your hoard the archaic verticals.

7

As you grow so comprehensively down to it
Is the world terrible?
Are our voices insect-wings?
Do memory's glints humiliate?
When we leave do unsilhouetted tides resume?

8

Marooned hump under white sheets,
all but the last questionable
letter of permission cancelled,
what an irreducibly modest claim for space,
what a Russian winter's stary retreat!

9

One has only so many chances at certain sounds,
they go by. Those free passes into the centre
are cut off. There is now no path
towards you but these words, which despair
every inch of the way.

10

Here is my thought-shelter
Here the unthreaded images roam
Sunlight, Father, Book, Leaf
My breathing
My shoulder sharpening beside my eye

LONELYHEARTS

Gentleman, 50'ish, country-lover, invites
letter from lady the same, marriage
not *ruled out,* he writes,

    and here and there women recall
a bosky walk, light rain
over the fields, it was then
and could be nice again.

Or: *Widow, grown-up children, own house and car,*
seeks generous-hearted man who shares
her fondness for travel, serious respondents only,

    and gents who'd felt that their affairs
were set for good remember journeys through
the land, look at the photos on their desks,
they'd have to ditch all that, could store a few,
decide their hearts are large and
fancy they might do.

Pathetic, no question. To suppose
these bios, which economy, so much per line,
has made stripped poems of, can land
them where the drift and wash of detail
will not reach, is plainly daft, and
answering them's a no less tranced denial
of their own impromptu, veering lives.

Though it may bring husbands and wives
this can't bring what they're after,
or not for long:
the hollows that lie between
these rudimentary peaks are what misled them

once, and though in nineteen
words or less they show they know
what went wrong then—
—that paltry, unbudged heart,
the shrill, reiterated disinclination
for the boring rural stroll—

—the roll
of unshared "interests" keeps untested
hazards still, and what seems worst
now may seem, next time round,
only what came first.

   Still: can all these poets,
forced by the high cost of language
into such calculated dreams, be wrong?
Suppose that one or two, and maybe these,
have finally got it straight (the words,
that is), so when she comes along,
or he, they'll be just
what the doctor ordered or the advert asked,
and will, because they must,
forsake all freer-ranging sounds, past
pledges, richer vows and subtler talk
to cleave to these few only, paid-for
covenant that will be manageable at last,

and so will, henceforth, hold fast to
            walk
in the country, keep a more
generous heart, to that house
in that car return always
from fond travelling.

SAMPLING FROM A DIALOGUE

Stopping by the bedroom wall he says God
damn it Marge (if that's her name), we have been through
this forty thousand times now let's have a new
line, I need to hear something different, and this odd
and, well, obviously it's inflated, analogy comes into his mind
—Roland, at Roncesvalles, and *his* last long call—
and he stands where he happens to be, beside the wall
and waits, listening, he knows now he's waiting for some kind
of miracle, what's she going to say,
one of them always finds a consoling pose
and his feel all used up, and he tries to picture those
horsemen, bright lances, rescuing armies on the way,
and from the bed behind him she says *Well*
maybe there is just such a thing as
having enough of somebody,
breaking the rhyme,
and both of them stay where they are, too far
apart again, in a clarity neither of them expected or thought
they were making, and listen to
the catastrophe of time.

THE WORLD OF WRESTLING

(Acknowledgements to Roland Barthes, *Mythologies*)

Why we watch them is their excess,
also their meaty contempt for
complex roles. We can watch all night
and never be misled.

Their austerity of gesture though shallow
is a relief. Here to be ambivalent is
amateur, and 'teasing the mind past thought'
a sickly aim.

They do not want anybody's time wasted.
This one's noble, could be our
more manageable though swollen
 brother, soaks up sympathy

and unfair forearm smashes to the face
though time's been called. The other's
vile. Foreign, of gross or debased
physique, he struts

and bullies, bellows, runs
cringing for cover or the ropes when
sleeping justice wakes. Sometimes
for weeks on end

he's masked, in this floodlit space
what could be more depraved? When
he's beaten they'll take it off.
Imagine being there then!

Light without shadow invites
emotion without reserve. Trapped
in the obligatory most loathsome
hold, the 'flying scissors',
the 'Macedonian choke',
they lie, they languish, they prolong
their agony like a pause in music.
Thinly their dream of pain
stains the hall,

we wear it like a simpler, more
intelligible skin. Our boundaries
gather in. Here we are one, we are

in control. Everything that may be
known here, we know. On our way out,
villains jostle us.

GUIDE BOOK

(Acknowledgements to the *Guide Michelin*, the *Guide Bleu*, et al)

None of us failed to admire the crowded
ranks and tiers, 12th century iconic craftsmanship (*anon.*)
of the Portail Royal at Chartres, windows
like banners down the nave at Rennes, four stars,
we all traversed the 'pleasurable terrain'—that is,
uneven ground—approaching Pleine Fougères,
and approved the three forks, three beds,
no bath rating of the *Hôtel Berceau du Royaume*
outside the village there. We did not forgo,
where *grande route* 776 meets 176, the monument
Aux Morts pour la Patrie, 37 roadside crosses
as you mentioned, nor miss, at Bec-Hellouin,
the St.Nicholas tower, 45 metres high, where
the knight Herluin in 1043 A.D. exchanged
his charger for a vow. To say nothing
of the unremittingly, as you note, picturesque
paysage between all these, frugally symbolized
by two stars, one hill, three trees. On your side
please permit me to record the small person
(also, it is customary, *anon.*)
observed sunning herself on the tidal rocks
at Mont-Saint-Michel, *clair-obscur* of her still
sun-warmed delicate body in the late afternoon
at the *Auberge des Puits de Bretagne*,
one bed, two baths.

Think what we like of him, dim old dawdler,
Main Street gazer, birdy shuffler—
stiff-collared, shiny-shoed—
or say it, his peace won't budge. He'll summon
our dead betters in dozens to smile us down,
they know if we don't who was there in livelier times
and did his share, helped give a shape
to shouts all hushed by now, and what's more
they won't change their minds. That time
the railroad almost picked another town, meetings
all night that week, and if you were there you heard
a few words from him, you bet you did; two wars,
 one that he went to; and everybody's climb, not easy, after
the market bust in '29. And in a pinch, what about
Jack Thwaite, the curling rink that night, and
what *he* said? Spare with his praise, Jack Thwaite,
so everybody heeded. They don't come
any fairer than Jack, and not saying this
on account of his fine sentiments that night, either.
Felt that way about him for years.
                                    And one or two
girls, never mind them, when he was a stripling,
before Clara. But he remembers a woman
getting out of a car in winter, must be
fifty years ago, wore a little fur coat and
looked him straight in the eye when he came up.
He kept right on going, of course, but
boy, was *that* a look!

WILLIAM, ETC

William, Percy, Fred, George, Pawcel and Jack,
all brothers and all relatives of mine,
all bearing the Coles name and all lost at sea
on the same ship, same day, in the '14-'18 War,
too drenched for graves so six names on a plaque
in a rural Somerset church, the usual
one-line *überschrift*, stonecutter's irony,
"Their Name Liveth For Evermore"—
would have been my uncles, once or twice removed,
if that day hadn't removed them before.

Think of all the cousins I might have had, and places
to be the caller-from-abroad in; or unfamiliar
anniversaries that girls who, old or dead now, may
have had to learn, and children's shapes and faces
hardly at all the same. Cancelled names on county
mailboxes, too, absences everywhere, you could say—
except for Davy Jones and those old watery arrangements,
what a jostling under 'C' that day!

GULL LAKE, ALTA.

"You just go out the door"
she said, "and it's down there to the right.
Not a lake at all,
just a pond, really, but
lovely after supper.
Uncle Bert would walk down
with white towels when it was
dark. *Once more across and back,*
we'd call. He'd wave, and leave
the towels on the bank."

Her old body
couldn't manage a dozen strokes now, and she's
three provinces away.

Those white towels on the bank!

AT THE SUNDAY TIMES' EXHIBITION:
"THE VICTORIAN FAMILY IN PHOTOGRAPHS"

I

They stand so familiarly everywhere, wearing
their usual clothes, unsuspecting how the sunlight
will thicken over them. Behind them, trees
which even then always grew over the shady places.

II

Children and grownups and dogs, standing or strolling.
Time has piled the sunlight along their limbs
and voices, it has hardened the margins around
their last movements and sounds.

III

Stillness and silence—my old temptations!

IV

They have maintained their discreet undertaking.
Brightening from the developer's tank, at once
they composed their minds against restlessness.

V

Complex rapture of other times! Do these images
sadden, charm, because they're gone, even
those children, that coatless uncle, couple strolling off—
all gone into the implacable abyss?

VI

Because we were not there
to breach them, glimpse ourselves out past
the hardening margins, the encrusting sunlight, and,
against the well-understood rules, remember
what came next?

VII

Because here their lives are focused,
gathered, fused, or seem so? And this is
all we ever want?

ALWAYS ABOUT MY HAPPINESS
AND MY UNHAPPINESS

So Anna Karenina, idly asked
what she is thinking about, nakedly replies—
"Always about my happiness and my unhappiness."

She is in love, which simplifies.
Tell her the miles of road still
echo past; last year, in Italy,

the Della Robbias made her weep;
high up, over the fields which keep
the early mornings longest here,

the sky is turning blue and brightening;

across the hall, library-shelves burn with
life-reminding wisdom; in the St. Petersburg house
her children are getting dressed now.

Some day she will have breath for all this.

Each year the youngest ones, primary sights
of first day back in cottage country safely seen,
patrol off down the beach road among tall grass,
cooling cars, and their own dwindling voices
to check up on her, rattle a stone

off a shuttered window if that's their mood:
it usually is. Movements then behind grey
glass curtains in the loft—life, its *reductio,*
still going on. Chalk one up, another cold season
survived, for the District Nurse, the County Visitor,

Sanitary Inspector, or who can say what other
diminished, obscurely-working purpose. That
next-door cottage has changed hands again, we notice,
easy to understand though nobody else here ever sells—
she hangs on, cats, rubbish, east-wind smells and all,

insulated by age and junk from what's below: which is
us, our unregarded passages, and infinitely nearer her
(how near, surmisable minds can't grasp)
boxes of Latin Readers and notes from Commencement Day
speakers, *Thank you Mr.McLintock, all you taught me,*

admired progenitor who died in time. How could
he know, or an extrapolated mother, loony years
afterwards not their fault. Since then
the acrid cats and *this*, layered in sour cardigans,
wool socks, multiple musty dresses like

a smuggler in long hiding, occasional apparition
to the strayed evening children.
"This is the spade Father used to turn
the stream. He dug the trench here. He said,
Have you ever seen so much goldenrod?"

Plunging to danger with every line
he'd leave her notes saying
darling I'll love you forever, then
pocket them in time.

Or when he'd wake from
dreams of shaded rivers, coloured birds
and miles of greenery further on
and keep her naked for a week

wisely he'd spare her the poetry and turn instead
to her white rib-cage and its bobbling
breasts, the lovely mindless
hours ahead.

Now that time's caught
and passed them here he's learned
to be much bolder than he was before.
Shows all he writes and talks a lot.

MRS. COLLISTON

The poem is based on the truncated account of a divorce case as
reported on a yellowed and torn half-page of an unidentifiable
Ontario newspaper dated May 11, 1918.

The headline "Mrs. Colliston On Stand in Divorce Case
(Continued from Page One)" is where
my eye was caught, why I retrieved the crackling fragment
from the long-stored cellar trunk; sharing that space,
adverts, notably one for "Excellent Balbriggan Underwear
For Men, 35c, 75c, $1 Per Garment,

Come One, Come All, Might
As Well Wear The Best This Summer As Wear This Or That."
Mrs. Colliston, I have read your testimony carefully,
how Miss Myers, your cousin who was staying the night
complained of feeling cold, and sat
all evening on your husband's knee,

though you suggested, once, she take your shawl instead—
how he compared her to "a little merry doll"
and how, when you retired, all three
slept in one bed:
which, when counsel asked if this were usual,
"Scarcity of bedclothes prompted such a move", you said.

Who would suspect that people could behave so ill?
Later, when you awoke, you heard those
"occurrences and conversations" close beside,
and when you turned on lights the two were still
embracing. At which Miss Myers rose
and left the room, you following, to comfort her, you testified.

Next day they kissed each other "frequently", were *seen*
to do so, this leading you to "institute proceedings"—
which is where your story ends for such as we
who were not there on May the 12th, 1918.
Yet not ends quite: for if I may, your grave deportment,
guileless manners merit some late comment still from me.

Dear Mrs. Colliston, although I search I'll find
no more Continueds from Page One
in this else-boring cluttered trunk
which your genteel story all these years has lined:
but I must tell you I admire none
here but you, I see you rise like Venus from the junk

made small and safe by time, if not by art,
a blameless miniature beauty, Mrs. Colliston,
all vulgar background noises died away.
The declaration's late, but from my heart
I love you, almost, Mrs.Colliston,
worth two Miss Myerses any day.

Since, though, I cannot meet you back in 1918, June,
when, as I deeply hope, your life
re-found its private, modest way,
I'll wish you better companions, no more cousins, and soon
a trusting, faithful gentleman who wants a ditto wife.
One note of warning, though, if I may

without offence: insist,
next time, on roomier quarters, if any
then discreeter guests, and finally, God knows,
should cousins call, and these have kissed,
let it be goodnight only, and be sure you've many
back-up bedclothes.

P.S. As for that husband who long ago
for the proprieties
showed so little care,
I'd only like to know,
though perhaps you're not the one to tell me,
did he remove his excellent balbriggan underwear?

"Fear of an odd sort", the Guardian's weekly essay
tells me, is what I'm bound to feel when
contemplating my child: this is because
what I now love will change, grow up, on some date
leave for events withheld from me, and even more surely
leave to become that adult for whom my tenderness
may not be rightly preparing. "Odd" indeed,
I reflect, standing pajama-bottomed at my bedroom window
after my late read, to acknowledge a "fear"
that such changes, small accumulating competencies
I admire and warm to, prophesy loss—
the much-debated first overnight away a signal
of unconsulted movements ahead, a sidling closer to
irreversible opaque time.
    Ironic, though, to see brimming
out there, now and years off, a love-sanctioning condition
neither of us, the way these matters seem to be arranged,
is likely to know how to intervene in—
and to know that my child won't really merit my least odd,
my most ordinary fear, until she's grown, on her own, and
watchful like this in sleepless, silent-windowed night.

NOT JUST WORDS BUT WORLD

Not just words but world grows simpler
as she dies. Now so much of what
subtly loured or beckoned, the nightmare's
endless stumble or the threaded maze to favour,
obliterated. Gone the mornings and thousands
of afternoons, puzzle of years, patternless
after all. Now it's just a straight dash
for the dark, so late the wasteful agendas
of expectation laid by.

Only the small ones, perpetual, remain. Now
she's sure she should have sat, chin in her hand,
watching her son's new eyes move, the sunlight
on the floor; with untrammmelled mind
more amply entered the early words; heedful
the smile for every homecoming. Does it matter?
Yes. Her daughter on the favourite roan pony,
cantering past, straightbacked and intent—
for that one, never such rapture since. Nothing
even close. Leave him, she should have told her,
all the bleak years. Of course she should,
and was so near to it so often. But
were all those nights like this one,
through her bedroom window slow fields of stars
up there? Those too. Those too.

"IF A MAN GOES PAST THE GREAT JOYS WHICH LIFE PREPARES FOR HIM..."

–L.N.Tolstoy, *Resurrection*

Seldom a matter of choosing, simply that which
you do not enter. You go past. Which perhaps was
great joy.

Street you do not walk down, town you incuriously
bend from. Centuries of aimed motions at last
peaking, exact architecture attentive.

Page you do not turn, words intimately
crafted. Girl whose dismissed body
is hazardous forever.

          *Verweile, verweile doch, Du bist
so schön,* you then recite—
Will not *verweile,* not stay.

Woodsman on northern lake. Creak of oar-lock,
oar-plash in repetitive, life-lapping
seasons.

   A way of staying,
of not going past. Not for me
to judge.

Patience of parks in glance-filled cities.
Those voices in languages unlearned,
part-learned, words longing

to be understood. A man goes past
and declines to go past. He posts look-outs
and listeners. He puts his past

to his ear like a conch, his lives
clamour, they have gone on.
And he goes on.

  And stays, stays,
so fair. And all
go on.

PHOTOS IN AN ALBUM

They are like pools. The surface
of these prints shimmers,
while just below
he and his friends, intermittent swimmers,
hide in gliding time, or rise
showing changing faces as years pass.
He'd dive here again if he could, or here, eyes
wide open now, and this time swim
deep down to perfectly know
everything between:
his life's confidential flow.

RUNNING CHILD

Watching my running child
on her seventh summer's beach
I see that other child
incredulously allowed back
through the afternoon's haze
to run beside her,
turning his head towards her
to gauge his joy

thirty years ago.

NOSTALGIE DE BONHEUR

J'ai appris qu'on est plus malheureux
dans le malheur que dans le bonheur
  —Armand Salacrou

Having been down myself more than I like
even if so far never quite out,
and finding no shortcuts to up

just having to sweat it through,
and usually losing weeks
in the process

Noticing to my soul's chagrin
that at such times even
the truly superior wisdom

of favourite authors is no help,
neither are my notebooks,
jottings recording

against just such emergencies
the endured loneliness
of admired men,

passages of real sustenance and
understanding when encountered in
less baleful hours,

it now seems time to admit that
nothing is so much to be avoided
as unhappiness,

a perhaps obvious conclusion
except that I have not always
found it obvious,

imagining that essential discoveries
were to be made down there,
down there in unhappiness,

a received idea, no doubt,
from an adolescent and boring
source, certainly one only

marginally borne out
in my own life, which has had
enough of it now,

enough time wasted in the dark service,
and desires now to announce
a late switch (there is nothing

precocious about me),
from now on I'm for happiness,
at least it's

a well-documented
ambition, my new slogan is
Down with *Weltschmerz,*

the moon is more beautiful
through the strayed curtains
of a man who knows this much

than it is over all Asia.
I'll see how it turns out.

ON A BUST OF AN ARMY CORPORAL KILLED ON HIS TWENTY-FIRST BIRTHDAY DRIVING A MUNITIONS WAGON IN THE BOER WAR

In Port Elgin, Ontario

Ten feet up atop a slim stone column
his face, neatly bearded, forage cap
tidily centred, stares out over the town's
bowling green. His modest demeanour precludes
any phallic reference—Freud's coeval,
he is innocent of much that we have agreed
to know. This summer he has been here
eighty years. Beneath him, now as in most
summer evenings all this while, 80-year-olds
in straw fedoras and roomy trousers trundle
their bowls up and down the trimmed and floodlit
lawns. Their ages seem as unchanging as his,
their conversations are of the seasons and the fields,
their fashions a matter of apparent obdurate
conviction. For eighty years their random
old-folks' wisdom, their windy laughter,
cautious gaits, have entered his vision, risen
to his hearing from these murmurous lawns.
Winters some die, turn, though not here, to stone
as he did, replacements take over. This summer
a few of them might, finally, have been his unborn
children. Late at night he sees these enter
the soundless green, begins to hear the suppressed
click of bowls, the floated discreeter voices. And
finds it odd, still, those distant, paused horsemen,
that roaring hurt, reins gone slack,
in Africa.

EARLY MORNING

Based on an August 13, 2000, newspaper item

Every morning, early every morning
he walks down an avenue of elms
and across a small field
to Donnington parish church, of which
he is vicar, and there he "prays,
in solitude". Simple repetitive act
which asks no complex comment,
which like a ship in the deep,
like ribbed snow in night-wind,
like love, deserves to escape
the diminishing visitation of words.
This morning at seven, nearby
or a thousand miles from you,
he'll walk down the avenue of elms,
across the small field,
he is there.

In the ballroom of the Schonbrunn Palace
the *corps de ballet* of the Vienna Opera
is dancing the *Kaiserwalzer* to lush vistas
of the almost endlessly banked and tiered
violins of the Vienna Philharmonic. Not
merely their own apprenticeships
(thousands of rehearsal and performance
hours of dancers and musicians) have
fashioned this moment, but generations
of predecessors may be glimpsed here too,
borrowings from minute, pure motions
attempted and debated and noted and
sometimes, when deserving, incorporated
into orthodoxy. Not to mention these
gold-laquered walls, lucent mirrors,
an infinity of multi-faceted crystal teardrops
in light-teeming chandeliers, all these
immersed now in this *Urquelle* of
lavish Straussian sound, clear echoings of
the younger Johann in his adoring imperium.

Among all these how easily have appeared
the *de luxe* white bosoms of the girls
in the *corps de ballet,* effortless revelations
of opulent Hapsburg centuries, observant
Hapsburg taste. Everything here
is secretly designed to honour them—
the room, the music, me.

THE PRINZHORN COLLECTION (1982)

THE PRINZHORN COLLECTION

Verwaltungsdirektor
Alte Staatsgalerie
München, 18 Januar, 1981

…Finally, let me kindle your
curiosity a little (may one say
'kindle'? I am grateful for any
corrections!) concerning our current
exhibition here. After *Der Blaue*
Reiter, so great a draw in the fall,
We have now—drawings, letters and
Journals by the inmates of a 19th century
Irrenanstalt (madhouse)! A worthy
doctor named Prinzhorn salvaged these
during his own tour of duty there
from the disregarded files of
a predecessor. *Mein Lieber*,
they are strong stuff.

The women's drawings, *zum Beispiel.**
You would suppose it an assigned
school-exercise, so alike, soon so
almost-routine, are these fantasies!
The women picture themselves always
naked; very often kneeling; and time
after time their faces, averted from us
and curtained by manes of long, long
hair hanging down their backs—can it be
that it was never cut?—are pressed into
the unbuttoned flies of a plump,
moustached and be-medalled policeman.
The shaft of whose erection is occasionally
visible, in part of course. And who stands
impassive, stolid, unstartled. He expects
this. It is either his duty, or his right.

------

*for example

One thinks of Edvard Münch's women,
so often seen from the rear, their backs
a gleaming whiteness down which
a dark river of hair, a wide, slow curve
of it, flows; their mouths similarly
glued, of course Münch was called
mad too. I have always felt uncertain
about that. Doubtful. I still do. But
it is another, possibly deeper, layer now,
is it not? I can hear you saying so!

Over the men's drawings here I draw,
not without predictable awkwardnesses,
a veil. As for the journals, the letters:
they record termless time. Complaints,
threats, fawnings, explanations, excuses,
prayers. Rational and irrational proposals.
Traüme und Alptraüme, dreams and
nightmares; the latter, literally translated,
'mountain-dreams'—a more powerful image
there, would you agree? No? "Ah, these
Germans", you murmur instead, "how
they love powerful images!" Let us pass
uneasily on. In short, an entire human-condition
is here, everything except utter despair.
Verzweiflung schreibt nicht, we say—
despair doesn't write. But from the borders
of despair, yes. Often, it seems. It is
the address from which many of these
dispatches are mailed. *To* nowhere. Only
to the Herr Direktor's pedantically-indexed,
whisper-free files.

...Nowhere until now. And what strikes one
now, browsing through these derelict
100-year-old signals (airless cries, unlit
gestures) and with the bureaucratic moiety
of the dialogue at last, blackest of ironies,

not getting through, is that these writings
have the uncontested rhythms of truth. As if
after so many years muzzled very far down
in the dark, they have become transparent
and are unable to hide anything. And gazing
right through these transparencies, one sees
oneself. Choking.

Joseph Grebing. I could choose others,
I shall name only him. A dozen letters, almost
all to his father. Also a stupendous, illuminated
scroll, like a page from a Book of Hours, but
this one single-track, single-authored,
self-memorializing, and this self running nose-down
for redemption, breathing audibly, even panting;
the scroll hand-drawn and coloured in reds and blues,
more accurately in crimsons, lapis lazulis, indigoes;
listing Joseph G.'s academic honours, which although
modest are set down with *élan*, with *punctilio;*
and his unsullied *Herkunft* (pedigree, provenance);
and his outraged innocence. Yes, 'outraged'—this
document, at first glance merely a more vivid replica
of those ornate confections to be seen on the walls
of rustic solicitors, all penmanship and pomp and
the signatures of hapless mini-dignitaries, on closer
inspection reveals a smuggled sub-text. A thin,
leaf-coloured tendril winds from one beflowered
upper-case letter to the next, and contains, like
an icon'd saint's girdle, messages—to speak plainly,
just one message, of unmistakable awfulness.
A message four words long, the four words repeated
over and over along that tendril's curlicued length,
ending where they begin and beginning again
where they end, and so elegant and near-runic in
design as to mislead the eye into believing them
there for the design's sole sake. This at-length
deciphered rune reads: *Du hast keine Idee Du hast
keine Idee Du hast keine Idee.*

Du hast keine Idee.

You have no idea.

The cunning of the workmanship, which
at first disguises, when found out enhances
the hysteria.

But I anticipate. It is not until his eighth
institutionalized year that this scroll engrosses
Joseph. Meantime, the letters.

"Geehrter Vater,
Ich weiss nicht, ob Du vergessen hast,
*Dass Du einen Sohn hattest…"**
—this is written six months after
his arrival. He is 31 years old. He will
continue writing letters until he is 43,
after which we know nothing more. He
stops. Simple. Chaos drinks him.
Drawings accompany many letters,
they continue until the forged opus
described above (his Chartres, his
angelic host, his thousand-mouth'd
Cry of the Innocents), then cease. What
do the drawings show? Himself in
pastoral attitudes. A repetitive but not
disagreeable series. He is usually wearing
a lemon-coloured short-sleeved shirt, and
gazes directly out at us. Among haystacks.
By a stream. Tending sheep. Look,
he seems to say—while you watch, while

------

*Honoured Father,
I don't know if you have forgotten
That you had a son…

you walk by, I am here. While you
accomplish the seasons of your life. And yet,
*und doch,*the ubiquitous small figure appears
to be assuring us, See, I am good. I am small
under the blue sky. In my lemon-coloured
shirt, I am no trouble.

What do you think,
Lieber Freund, what is your professional
judgement? Do you suppose this is so?
Does the colour of his shortsleeved shirt
tell you this is how he is? Or do you suppose
this is not he at all, in this yellow shirt, turning
his button eyes towards us beside the unmolested
stream—?

Perhaps they thought, the doctors,
the rapt curators of so much *Entartete Kunst,**
that it is a trick. An eight-year hoax! In this
yellow shirt there is nothing more than
a harmless *Doppelganger*, set going by
a madman's brush. While the madman himself
watches touchily, wrathfully, from the shelter of
a neutral tint.

"Father: This is the second year I write
to you at this season—"

"Father: Although I confess I was ill at ease
during all that month and thus disturbed
my fellow-workers, your employees,
for which I again apologize, still I did not

---

*a phrase coined by the Nazis to characterize Art unacceptable to
the regime ('artless' or 'malformed' art, approximately); thus, most
non-representational art, Picasso, Max Enst, and certainly most of the
drawings in the Prinzhorn Collection

deserve this. It is too much. The noise
at night here, you have no idea. The *Gestank.*
The people."

Or to his brother Paul. No one had visited him
that year, either. Or, for all he knew, or we know,
written.
"*Lieber Paul:* There is no good ground, merely
because I am taking no part in the business,
to ignore me. How willingly would I set forth
in the mornings beside you—"

Here is the last letter, written when he is 43.
"For the twelfth year I write at Christmastime.
I hope and pray you are well, also my mother.
I enclose a drawing of the scene I can so well
Imagine—"

This crayoned drawing survives. One sees
that it was folded four-square, then once more,
to fit an envelope. A well-dressed man
sits in his parlour, hands clasped upon the head
of a walking-stick, seeming to approve as
a woman and several daughters decorate
a tree. One of the girls is standing, in
a long skirt, on a stepladder. Both her arms
reach up towards the top of the tree, where
she is fastening a star.

Finis Joseph Grebing, at least my account
of him. His testament—the above-listed
artefacts—was, as I have said, found in
the Herr Director's *Büro.* Nothing of it
was ever mailed, or we should not now
have it. The drawings. The letters. An
illustrated calendar, of which I may say
more when we meet. The self-portrait,

or, as it may be, the *Doppelgänger*,
he of the lemon-coloured shirt.
The certificate, icon, scroll, with
the leafy tendrils. *You have no idea.*
Along with the memorabilia of other
long-stay guests or personnel,
cf. that odd business of the guard,
as he undoubtedly was: moustache,
prick, shiny medals, paunch.

A final ironic touch. The admirable
and eponymous doctor, Prinzhorn, has,
In a brief catalogue entry, the following
dates attached to his name: 1887-1933.
He seems to have been a humane man,
or he would not have been so struck (so
'stricken', I am almost sure I should say)
by his discoveries among his predecessor's
files, and we at the Galerie would have had to
seek out other images to hang on our walls
this New-Year season. This humaneness
admitted, one is bound to feel Doktor
Prinzhorn timed his death wisely. To have
soldiered on even a few years longer
would have meant risking learning worse news
still, and hearing an even more massive cry.

One would not wish him that, God knows.
Indeed, on either humanitarian or divine grounds
one would not wish God that. Though presumably
He already has it, has learned all and heard all,
never mind what one may wish.

Enough. *Basta*, the amateur metaphysics.
Not for me to meddle with. I return, stooping
a little, towards my competency, the visible.
The Prinzhorn Collection moves to Dusseldorf

in March, there are no plans for it after that,
it will be dismantled. A sculpture exhibit
is due here from Berlin at that time—
two young artists, a married couple in fact.
I know little of them. Perhaps you will come,
your students will be nice, they will allow you.
We willl talk. Yes? Try. This long letter,
Sorry. More *sangfroid* next time. I am
sorry for this.

NO ONE THERE

Until he was five his body
in intermittent observed perfections
showed what he would grow to.

His face sometimes confided it.
A guest, seeing him led
from the grownups at bedtime, felt

unaccountably moved and said so,
though this was received awkwardly
and the moment petered out. Still,

his parents had their thoughts,
kept counsel, school happened and
those years rose about him

as unachieved as always, there was
a gradual settling for merely good
news, love not exactly lessening but

as though, their feeling was,
that greater air was near also
for us, the world mutable once, and

now we see it hovers again
for him but look, it seems lifting
past, just out of reach,

well it was always likely.
Meanwhile this is not so, no,
he is in it, he breathes

a deep gust of the world and
it is easy but they do not know,
they are too old now.

What was the point of it,
he wonders, he is afraid
he has dawdled.

True, several years admiring women,
in retrospect stereotypical
splendeurs et misères, but even so

it is hardly his fault
it is just the way things are
people do not wait long enough.

Just when you turn towards them
saying, Look, see how I have
drawn or coloured this,

and saying, Uttermost joy need not be
dissembled, this has been judged
pretty good by many,

and also, at last, confessing
I have done it mostly for you,
there is no answer

there is no one there
it is disquieting
you knew this would happen but not yet

and dead mothers and fathers
cruise impassively
in the luxury cabins and

fragrant seas of children
rich, whatever form that takes,
a little too late.

'AH! QU'ILS SONT PITTORESQUES, LES GRANDS JARDINS MANQUÉS!

Laforgue can have his trains—
what brings the yearning arrow
on its long arc into me anytime
is nothing so down-the-platform-dwindling
but is the naming of the great public gardens of central Europe—
Mirabelle, Prater, Englischer, Kravlokà.
These names control entire decades of drifting
shade and sun, while beyond them
cars with absurd and tiny accelerations
fret the historic perimeters:
Salzburg, Vienna, Munich, Prague.
What are they, the great gardens, except
unhurried and beech-avenued and
bronze-dignitary-supervised, but
every now and then in an unselfconscious hour
one of them, Mirabelle, say
(and should Prater or Englischer ever do this
at the same time it is terrible, wasteful,
awful) can release into a carefully thought-about
place a woman whose beauty
seriously stuns a region of the blood
of any *flâneur* who sees her. And this
of course is why that blood-stunned man
is here, and why, years ago,
he was in a similar garden in Dresden and
Leipzig too, sometimes with a Russian name
in those far-off and inequitable days
and sometimes French or German or English
but most often, probably, Austrian (although
this matter of national avocations
remains of undocumented significance here),
entering the park in the sunshine

in the early afternoon for the park's own sake
though bearing his composed hope or
expectation with him, and the park
opening itself to him, its straight avenues and
its fountains, their plumes of water
chugging thinly upwards between the sunlight
and his eye, and its well-raked walks and
its oddly complaisant rain-simplified horsemen.
And the woman, in the randomly-occurring long
afternoons when one of the women is there,
turns her unguarded face, her unbearably
though from our intact points of view
blamelessly beautiful face almost towards him
in some moment when he is about to reach
the fountains in the park's centre, and sometimes
he speaks to her
with sublime consequences and sometimes
her beauty seems all at once too unmanageable
for any words of his and then
he may find instead a shopgirl showing
smooth knees on a bench, and there are
ample justifications for this. I have been in
all of those gardens I have named,
although the gardens in Dresden and Leipzig
I have not been in.

                    Krailling, bei München,
                    Dez. 1980

ABRUPT DAYLIGHT SADNESS

Abrupt daylight sadness of one to whom
a small child says, "I love you
more than anybody else in the world."
This is a father or a mother, usually—
at once they know there is nothing more to want here
forever, he knows this, she knows this,
they fly a short way towards real Heaven
but soon knowing it is more than they may
have or should desire, pause and fall
back. Sharp arrows from one too young
to know Time, the enemy.

ABANDONED LOVER

Whether he rushes vainly, or
crawls to weep, she is there.
In his belly or ribs she may
any minute begin again that walk
towards him, wearing that dress.
Her voice knows a hundred ways
to start. Along his forearms, perhaps,
her naked body surges in their
last lovemaking. Probably
this is worst. No, worst
is remembering she is somewhere,
doing new things.

AND CANNOT DISPEL THE DARK

To everything that unwatched and alone
survives,
a bush at night beside a wall, a stone,

beasts of the field who stand
in webs of rain
when webs of blowing rain turn all towards dark and

all are lost from sight
in the countryside's obliterating,
light-slaughtering night,

and to all who find their way
from extinction-goading singleness at evening
into a next day,

and to your breasts, sequestered from common view like all these
and cannot dispel the dark, but,
pale symmetries

below me and exigent when closely above my mouth and eyes,
and swift in attendance, make short work of all
night-time *angst*, obscurophobia, morbid reveries.

This thin spatter of words on a page
bringing snow, for example, into
close juxtaposition with your glimmering

breasts, harms nobody. Gladdens me
with domiciled you, pricks this one
from his rented room onto, he hopes,

cordial streets, allows that other a wintry
glimpse. But here is also the French
film director asking, inside his movie,

what marriage means to a woman.
Pretty girl: "*C'est donner ses seins
et ses jambes.*"

This is confusing, but only a little.
Being both graphic and reductive, it allows
a sort of thrill through. Believing

that most of us feel this (the *frisson,*
I mean), I have to think nobody much
comes out of this creditably.

EARLY LOVE

One afternoon *à propos* of something
I have lost track of, she asked me
did I know much about Catholics. Almost
crippled with joy at this sign of
spirituality I at once borrowed
from the local library the two volumes
of Ranke's *History of the Popes*, which
as luck had it no one had signed out
since July 12, 1932. How those blue spines
crackled when the covers were bent back flat!

NATALYA NIKOLAYEVNA GONCHAROV

(She will marry, on February 18, 1831,
Alexander Sergeyevich Pushkin)

Another of the placid beauties! Whose
mother flaunts her before the poet—
clamberer among words, his monkey-trellis
of language, toxic dexterity. It is all he has.
Le pauvre, c'est déjà trop. Her white skin,
if he would stop here where others have
but, ah, imperial softnesses in her blouse,
the swelling, shaded baskers. Who could
ask for more? *Than two?* Hear how
last year's irreverence now falls short.
His words against that same restraining
silk her soft body butts—of course
it's no contest. Inside her head, not
a sound. Instead, a shape, shapes within
shapes, her stately shoulders, a mirrored
torso half-turns, ripples whitely. These
forms both mimic and predict his dreams,
which have no other guides. Try arguing
with that! Her thighs, proffered, see, see,
on the low divan where they stream.
They are endless as Homer. The light
slides on them, firmpacked emblems,
serene martyrs. To pour images is fine,
drowning in them however is no joke.
Onegin, of course, had the same problem.
Or think of, inside *his* huge story, Pierre
Bézuhov: Hélène, brainless, as he knew,
but mitigatingly décolletaged, bending
towards him over the dinner-table, *déesse!*
World-altering. And now Natalya

Nikolayevna offers her word-monkey
"Her whole body only veiled by her
thin grey gown." At which all roads
out of this place—gone! Until death!
Because what a place it is, for a poet.
"Her whole body"—and all of it
dumb. Amazing. No rhymes but are
his own. *Odalisque, risque.* All directions
to this lavish property, his. Such white
abundance. Her thighs. She "doesn't like
poetry". When they. When she opens
them. Ah. The Church. Bless it. Soon.
Can she talk?

IN GAMLA STAN*

*Old Town

Awful, I guess, how,
without knowing why, I should
at different stages of my life
be addressing this person or that
so often, idling among
sleeps at night or earnest explanations
driving alone in the car, and how
just now, for a month or two, it's
you, woman approaching me
along Västerlanggåtan in the Old Town
in Stockholm, your figure under your dress
like a lucid white fish swimming up close
to the surface and disabling my mind
for minutes then and random, stabbing
arrests long afterwards too,
     it's you I refer
my life to, twenty years later
what do you think, do you
approve of much, undarkening
white fish although lapping time
has covered you, you whom I
followed only as far as Stortorget
and who knew I was following but who
offered nothing, only your body's
white and patient bonding, lovely
undefended stride into the afternoon's
long composition,
     and who now, again,
here, halts me, stalls me now
mostly with stillnesses, small
gleams, dumbshows of happiness

—Västerlanggåtan, your dress
like thin water, silvering, and
disabling with impending
white—and holds out to me,
not for the first time it has been
held out to me
    that ruinous icon,
    bliss
you wordless judges, you glimmering,
perfect, deepsea listeners.

I LONG FOR PEOPLE THROUGH WHOM THE PAST*

Candleflame winks and flaps in early
afternoon. Sparkles, on the silver-crammed
sunstreamed dining table, the crystal.
Crimson-rimmed Limoges the multitudinous
reflecting surfaces incarnadine.

The gifts have been opened and are
ours. Here, for the family
entering now through the double doors
from the hall, entering the heartland,
is no anxiety.

I scan an adored scene. Gran's.
Christmas Day, the long dining room.

Watch them gather. My grandfather, poised
to carve. He hates this job. So small
behind the enormous bird you would
never know he's standing.

*"Debout, Duclos!" they cried ironically
at the Vel d'Hiver a dozen years later when
the stumpy Party Secretary peered, almost,
over the lectern. First days in Europe
and by no means understanding everything,
I laughed immoderately.*

Light veers off his thickish rimless
specs, careens about walls. He clashes
his knife tentatively, frowns at his
complacent, baked enemy.

---

* "...in its large lines, continues to be connected with us, related to us."
    —R.M.Rilke, *Letters*

My mother arranges the smallest ones.
I have arranged myself, I am ten, I
no longer sit at a table leg.
The room glitters. Like armour. Sometimes
the entering family are warriors crowding
onto the land. Out of the dragonships,
the darkflashed sea.

Twenty years ago I watched the lights
of Västerbro shine through a Stockholm
Christmas night from a flat high up over
the Mälar-sea. Windows open, Hary Janos
on the record player, that intermezzo circling
out and away through the high icy air. It was
all I cared about that night in that town.
A skinny egoist in a crystalline place.

Frank offers me a cracker to pull.
Reach in, he says, feel for the flap.
Hold tight, the bugger can slip. This
youngest uncle points out the celluloid
reindeer drawing sleighs full of jellybeans
past the children's places. Red runners
over the perfect linen.

Perfect. Everything that will happen today
will behave as though it is perfect.

In at the hall door, out again towards
the kitchen, a bird flies through the room.
Along the wall, effortless bird of light,
urged by my grandfather's rimless specs,
his turning head.

My 14th Christmas I imagined falling
in love. We walked on a summer evening
by the shore of a lovely lake. It was in

Switzerland. Beyond the lake, pale hills
shimmered. As we walked I gazed at her face
from the side. It was gentle and familiar.

Now watch the faces wink out. My
Gramp, now dead almost thirty years.
Gran appears in a quick shot, the year
after he died, my father carving now.
Gran gazes at us as though for two.

Here is my mother. For another minute
she attends to the small one beside her,
they are whispering, perhaps both laugh.
Then fades into her long last years.
A bed among slow dyings.

Frank, who later that hour alleged
I had held the wishbone too far up,
is the one who will let his car's exhaust
fill him up in his garage. I have never
allowed this outside my mind before.
Instantly the jellybean sleighs are driving
all over the place, some of them toppling
sideways.

Occasionally, not often, a face will remind
me of her. On the subway, a month or so ago.
On the TV once. The lovely lake begins to form
behind her. How do I feel then?

Bad.

And here is Mary, who should not be here
at all. Mary is my father's youngest sister,
who died of diphtheria when she was nine.
Long before I was born. So how did she
get here?

... Because my father touched
her cheek when he came home from school
one of her last days. He remembered
how warm it was.

Crimson the carrion, the sunless bodies
piled.

And I, who write this in a Christmas
season, am now fifty, and sit in my own
bright hall. All these recede, they are
long ago, the sun is off them. My
grandfather. My mother, nursed
through her too-long last years by
parodies of that lovely intelligence. My uncle,
who eluded all that, and us, in time. Mary,
warm-cheeked, by definition over-expectant
of the life waiting. It's now ten years since
my daughter said to me, "Tomorrow I'll be
eight. I'm getting older." I never listen to
words like those.

You look through the dark glass,
as you always have. What moves there
in a little light, and then leaves,
is all you know.

"Oh strange little intensities,
delicate odd links in the long
chain—sanctities, pieties,
treasons, abysses!" *

e.g.

My grandfather lying on his last
bed, staring ceilingwards. Behind
that motionless face, face dourly
hardly ever tilted down towards
a book, the lost libraries of Alexandria
burning again—

Great relief at being, during my third
decade, in cities where I had
nothing special to do. Avenues I could
stroll in all afternoon, or not. As if
not being known by anyone there
released me into some earliest self
who, being unknown, could feel
limitless everywhere—

Those cities: Florence, Stockholm,
Copenhagen, London, Zurich, Munich—

———
* from Henry James's Journal

Pearlbreasts of Ingres' Mme de la
Jonquière. Coercive sexuality of those
small swollen bellies perched up on
the skinny legs of the elder Cranach's
women (Venus, Eve...)—
Akhenaton disait: "Je suis heureux
d'être nè au pays des imbéciles"—

A photo dated 1910 showing factory-hands
walking home at dusk, some with slung
jackets and many, oddly, wearing white shirts.
Behind each of them another of those many
unseen corridors, *coulisses,* leading back into
faces turning, greetings somewhere familiar
and expected, and charged moments as when
he stumbled into love or fatherhood—

(I seem to love all of them. This
may be because they are all dead, all
gone without a sound; no final thoughts,
or fuss, or attitudes on the horizon. This
seems finer than any poem.)

Also, the white blobs against the indistinct
slum street remind you what splendid targets
they will all make in a few years—

The Portuguese chicken-coop girl—

She was kept in a chicken-coop all her
short life. Infant-size when discovered
at age ten; scuttled, scratched, 'talked'
like a chicken. The neighbours hadn't
wanted to interfere. Died shortly after
being rescued. She was there during
all of my third decade (Florence,
Stockholm, etc)—

The tribe called Caduveo in the Mato
Grosso believe that a magic animal,
touched by the immensity of their
sufferings and their prayers, will be
forced to appear to them and help
them—

The last entry in E.M.Forster's Diary.
"Have ordered the book (which goes to
the College Library) to go to the College
Library. How it rains!"—(How
insupportable, intelligence grown old!)—

1944, a railway station-master, explaining
to a visitor what the '*Süssliche Geruch*'
(sweet smell) is: "*Das sind die Toten
die hier in Auschwitz verbrannt werden*"—*

And more, of course; of course, much more.
A child's elbows and forearms digging into
warm sand on a cottage path after
the goosebumps of indoors; unsuitable
erotic attachments, everywhere you look
people perishing with longing at the wheels
of stationary or pointlessly driven cars, or
seated with open unread books before them,
pitons, holdfasts, all these, because
without them they will fall out of their lives,
out of their thirty, their forty, their fifty years,
into the simplifying wind—

Also, needless to add, a lot of days
that just faded out quietly—

---

* "Those are the dead, who are burnt here in Auschwitz."

This picture-book is still open.
One day, however, it will shut, and
a half-second before its facing images
collide, they may realize that great and
inexplicable changes await them; e.g.,
sitting with Forster in his rooms in King's
my grandfather, some grey afternoon in the 1930's,
will watch the endless East Anglian rain slant past
the long leaded windows; Venus and Mme de la Jonquiere
will contract submissively or sceptically their respective
softnesses into low-roofed pens; a magic animal will enter
Auschwitz and pad everywhere, everywhere—

But all, when death makes unperplexed
again, will separately rejoin the air and
earth. There can seem a kind of wastefulness
in this, hence the belief, among those
depressed by wastefulness, that somewhere
there must be a file....but, *que voulez-vous*,
nobody will miss, or miss half as much
as you will, these things you have seen. It is
what happens to picture-collections.

MAJOR HOOPLE

A grotesque, I knew.

Vainglorious and logorrhoeac, gassing away
from above his ballooning waistcoat
to lodgers sitting or standing in
attitudes of decorum-annulling scepticism.

He seemed to have no teeth; neither did
Martha, dirigible-wife. Their identical faces
were puddings. Hers was sensible and without
illusions. Two or three times a years she would
almost smile.

His harrumphing and egadding.
His fez. His spats.

The skinny boarders, travelling salesmen
by the unpremeditated look of them.
Proofs of their lostness were the lengthening
cigarette ashes, wilting towards
rumpled shirts. They had nobody
to warn them.

To what did I compare him? To
a home-derived image of man as
unmockable, the high seriousness
of middle years. By which standards
he would not do. So gross, so
little respected. He verged on
the repellent. He was barely human.
He was appalling.

But now he fills me with longing
for a safe and reliable time where
he meant all those things—and
age and failure too, star-distant then
from me as those—instead of
a caricatured but incontestable man.

And where beyond him, and beyond
the afternoon paper's large pages,
the smell of newsprint coming up close
as my arms spread wide to begin the last
orderly re-folding, the lights have just come on
in the dining room. Soon a lost voice will say
come to supper.

THREE TOLSTOY POEMS

I. MISHENKA (in two versions)

I

At sixteen, Niki, Leo's father-to-be, got,
from his parents, a Play-'n-Learn
present: that is, a servant girl, who taught
him the necessary, and in return
became pregnant. This meant Niki was all right.
At least at night.

The baby, however, Mishenka, who, as fate
had it, lived, and grew up to become a kind
of stable boy, later coachman, on the family estate,
left, strange to say, not a wrack behind—
strange, I mean, when you compare
the marvels his half-brother left. Although their

lives *did* diverge. This older one, who, as somebody said,
had a "brutish" face, couldn't ever even have read
W & P, being illiterate, and he died
a pauper, two good reasons so far to decide
not to leave any messages—so if he forgave
the family, if he felt, ever, it had been more worry at how he'd behave

than real honest-to-God hardness of heart or unconcern,
well, we can't tell. The fact is, from such
as Nicholas Tolstoy's oldest son, we will learn
nothing of any of this. Or not much.
Something about sadness. Something that sinks
the heart a bit, is all. The rest's gone missing.
There's not a photo, or parting word, nothing to show what he thinks
about his child, if he ever had one. Nobody reminiscing.

II

At sixteen, Leo's father got
a present from his parents.
Sort of Play-'n-Learn.
This worked out pretty well.
Meanwhile the present,
a servant girl, duly became
pregnant, had Mishenka.

Mishenka, although older than Leo
and, of course, his half-brother,
never exactly became Leo's
alter ego,
no,
he hung around the stables mostly,
did not learn how to read or write,
became a groom when he was old enough,
developed a "brutish" face,
and to cap it all off
died a pauper. How's that for
dissimilar brothers?

II. A View from the Side

All he had to go on from the day when,
in his twenty-third month, his mother died,
was a framed silhouette in black paper,
the simplifying view from the side

the century favoured. This is still to be seen.
It shows the round forehead and chin of a little girl of ten,
and much more than this it's difficult to find there.
Her son, however, accepted the difficulties. Again

and again for the next eighty years
the revered novelist, prophet and finally saint
of Most of the Russias tried to breathe life
into this frustrating profile. Faint

echoes of endearments from him to her and back
show up in his journal, ghosts of strayed
appointments and misplaced *cris d'enfance*—
"*Maman, Maman,* hold me!"—but if she made

it up to him, ever, if her early vanishing
contributed, for instance, to that extra space
he always seemed to have had, that extra body-width that
lets us get our hypnotically close-up place

beside Bézuhov, or Levin, hear them marshalling
their rambling, noble minds, the journal doesn't say.
"I would, if I could, become a tiny boy,
close to my mother, the way

I imagine her", is what it says instead;
and, "My *Maman,* whom I could never call
that because I did not know how to talk when
she died." She remained, of course, through all

this, ten, the forehead round, the chin
uncomplicated, while he carried the heavy
thoughts of his great life across the fields
and years and into those many

notebooks that filled and emptied, filled and
emptied, like great lungs, breathing more
life everywhere but here, failing only this
face on a black coin, *Maman*, the longed-for,

longing of which he wrote,
"All this is madness, but it is true."
The face grew dark and calm with time. It did not
speak. It offered nothing, aside from the view.

III. November 9, 1873

One hundred and eight years ago
today, his youngest son, Petya,
six years old, died of croup.
The journal "My wife is
plunged in grief."

What is left of this scrapey,
low-roofed cough, this small, hot
face, ceasing?

—"The world and those who
sail in her are resilient."

—"OK. Whatever."

No, these may be left: shape
of a glimpsed face in Zurich;
glance from a car-window
in Rio; also, odds are,
silhouettes in the countryside
round about—Yasnaya Polyana—

And here, in Toronto,
one hundred and eight years
afterwards, one who reads of it,
for a few minutes
stares at the grief-plunge.

IBSEN STANZAS

I

They called on him in Rome,
this woman who it seems had
abandoned husband, children, home
back there in Norway—with
her lover. Didn't doubt
he'd approve. After all, the far-famed
door-slam. But nothing doing.
"My Nora went alone."

II

I think of the music sometimes
August Söderman wrote
for Peer Gynt's rhymes—
you won't have heard it.
Söderman played it often for the poet
who, O, loved it, he said
—Those strains again, O
    they come o'er my ear—
everything was set.
But then one day Söderman was dead
and the music couldn't be found.
It hasn't been found yet.
Ever. Think of that. All gone into the air, or into the ground.
Like Söderman. They got Grieg to do it over, or instead.

III

At seventy he stopped talking to kings—
in particular, the king of the Danes
who "got little response from H.I.",
a royal diary complains.
Although it was a case of first things
first, obviously: two hours
later, when a young girl
called at his hotel with flowers,
the old boy charmed her.
                            Which reminds me:
a hanger-on named Nansen claimed
that girls of "tender ages"
would be told a tale
in which, grown very rich, H.I. finds the
world's most luxurious ship, engages
a gipsy orchestra and sets sail
for tropic isles—inviting
only "A few good friends", he'd say,
"and you, dear one, whom I would hug and kiss."
    When he'd do the writing,
who knows? It was "all pathetic anyway",
according to Nansen—longings like this.
He must have been n.c.mentis,
according to Nansen. H.I., that is.

IV

It was to Uppsala that in the summer of 1877 he went
for his Honorary Doctorate of Letters, after which the carriage sent
by the Swedish King took him, in late July,

down to Drottningholm, which is a low-lying palace with a green
roof outside Stockholm, the literal translation being, "of the Queen,
the home", and the two cool white arms of which lie

along the water. Here there was a farewell celebration in the park
with 'illuminations', as these were called, after dark,
and I like to think of him watching these and thinking what I

know are by now unrecoverable, sunk or exploded, thoughts,
                              sitting probably in a cane-backed chair
brought out from the Chinese pavilion among the dark fir-trees there,
and finding it all pretty foolish, surely, but putting up with it, keeping
                              an eye

on things since it's likely that then no less than now the sight of a young
                              svenska blonde would please
a watchful old fellow, and one or two may have sat, their smooth
                              effortless knees
glowing in the fireworks, on the grass nearby.

Visits to the Gericare Centre

As you steadily—startled
into reverie only when
the spoon nearly misses
your mouth—munch your way
through supper,

strapped up straight and fed
from a mashed bowl,
your eyes concentrating
as if to force
a devoted, furious someone

to appear,
far-travelled ransomer
with whom you soon must also be
far and travelling
(not as I am,

shuttered with memory and
with repeated enterings of this
room, also with thinking
of how the staircase
to the parking lot will look,

of an impending book or recent
sex—and you *convenable*, soon,
in after-hours stasis,
unable to turn over but staring out
over rubbishing years:)

who, when you go, will
guard that whole winter I
never left my bedroom or
the snow my window-ledge, kept
home from school

an endless, unachieving winter
to begin again, out of
childish muse and dream,
this old, hard business of
meddling with time?

II

This ward of women's hands, waving.
this monotony of minute
brandishings of hands
half-remembering shapes of
important things,

this meagre raving along
white-bordered coverlets
your hands disregard,
your hands precede you,
they have resigned

from all this,
you have withdrawn their
services. These unwrappings
of familiar objects, feeling along
the sheet

for a trusted plate, stooped
buttonings against bygone winters and
old frozen playgrounds, all these
your hands ignore. Shrouded and
austere, your hands are

lighting candles on a table before
expectant friends, it is only
the conversation that looms
unsure and difficult. I tell you
none here will mind.

III

Leaning over your bed I feel
the vertigo of old age. Me,
nel mezzo like most babblers,
can tell contagion's here
and I have caught it.

It is the silence made by dyings.
Tempts with crumplings of
voices you have always, always
heard, dwindlings of embarrassing,
greying shapes—

who once, now run on
out of earshot, were
all the scuffling children.
Straggler on your white bed, you
annihilate by forgetting.

IV

There was a day when the leaves
were yellow under the rain,
not the very last leaves
but almost, you said what is
to be done

with this body, these legs that
trudge it here and there

to no purpose, when I compare,
you said, these purposes
with others, O

tiny and shameful,
it was a day when
many of the leaves were
a flat, soaked yellow
on the glistening black pavement

and you could still explain
what was going on, what was
happening, you could demonstrate
the wonders of a normal competence,
mine, say,

by your own slow-motion,
inexorable, sometimes even
comical
declension from it.
The driveway was

yellow with soaked leaves
and if you had ceased then
I would not be beginning, sitting
so near you here, to understand
the intimate cynicism of the world.

v

Your face is between two mysteries.
How death will be, your face
in sprinting patches rusts
towards it, it is wearing out
towards one mystery.

The other is just before
I was born, I have studied
the inaccessible sunlight
on the verandah when I was almost
there, your face watches

my sister who is three years old and
stands mildly within the sunlight,
its prodigious composure
has always eluded me.
This is the other mystery.

VI

Here are the concentrated moments,
like landslides, blocking forgetfulness.
Your uncle driving the cart
into an abandoned barn
in a rainstorm,

sitting beside him under
the drumming roof, the wind
leading great paths of rain
across the roof. Those
floods of sound

overhead, the two of you solemn there,
brimming with noise. Your
scared, eager enduring.
In a pause, the horse
shaking its harness.

In those years in your Townships
when you were always in a hurry
to get to yourself, filching from
every room's disarray
a paring of temporary order,

another sliver of readiness—
gazing into the years along
those long lines of air,
arming yourself for important
movements, the first words

like snow already fallen behind you,
and then around you, soon heaping
immoderate with choices—
that early hurry you had,
did there anywhere exist

the towering event to satisfy it?
Or how long ago did you know,
when did the face you
held towards limitlessness
turn, with only

a little surprise, towards
memory? The gaze scan round
in that only direction
infinite, crammed with images?...Well,
the image that's coming

may be trivial. Too prolonged, *this*
silence, to hope for raptures. Though
we may hear the pause in which life,
as if already leaving,
shakes its harness.

VIII

How human beings are alike
in undefended states!
No knowing how much you're
hearing or understanding, but
for an hour now

I have held your hand
and talked to you
of extreme things
—with silences between—
as you, in hours too early

in my life for me to give
accounting of, surely
with some comparable (privately
soaring) voice lulled or dreamed
me. As though we had,

those many years before,
leaned out to look and found
both of us (until both
faded there) listening from some
stupendous, covenanted

place to sounds too deep
for remedy. Those sounds are
burrowing but still audible,
it needs us both to
let them go.

IX

There is now no pleasure like
the pleasure of being alive then,
on that winter's day you skated

out along the Châteauguay
beyond the rim of houses
towards Aunt Sarah's, or I,
enough years on,
sped on the neighbour's rink
under the blue bulb swinging
at early dusk on its cord,

the ice sown with dazzle
like a Flemish pond, like
Cuyp's old silvering winters
below some dormant town.
How cold and clear

it shone, only the secret-keeping
child could tell—
to skate again that day,
joy would burst
our hearts!

x

There are no native speakers
of this dialect. But I allow your
mangled syllables to float towards
words inside me,
the slightest sound can do it.

What I'm afraid of learning here is
that the last images to fade show
accumulated secreted damage. If you
nod, if you even seem to agree,
I will absorb it as truth.

Words like 'worth', 'dignity', etc.,
circle this ward like planets.
If these words are not dead, if

those planets are reachable, they are for
moated and convoyed travellers.

Over the car-radio, report of
a white bear sighted forty miles off
Baffin, swimming away from land.
Tonight, driving towards you,
away from land.

XI

When a breath of early freshness
blows over you, even now
when a breath of a kind of
fullness re-opens the hiding-place
behind the leaves—

when he parted them
to find you hiding there,
even now when your young father
. parts the leaves,
always his face

bending close towards
thrilled laughter—
what kings, what legends!
Who is here now to find you
as you were,

who is here to find you before
the roamings into womanhood,
to find you among the leaves?
Press my hand if you know.
Press it anyway.

XII

What does the old chair
in your room, in the house which
I will but you will not
see again, think of you now?
How can your trusted books

bear other beginnings, the surfaces
of new eyes? Beauchamp in his career,
Lucy Gayheart's footsteps running
away, those journeyers who
wandered and for you

again and again wandered through
deepening Wessex hedgerows, these
go on, but now surely diminished, surely
interrupted as if by rain
in the middle

of a sentence. Those hedgecutters
who must now recollect
their craft alone and, stiffly
in rinsed landscapes,
start over.

"What is the good of having made
so many dolls?" Michelangelo asked,
and yet the stones he'd shaped brooded
near, that massive proof was
out in the light.

While you, whose wisdom's shut
and death's sheer edges all around,
slide traceless. Though there's
a narrow rim of calm. God help us
to our proper use.

XIII

Remembering that line praising
"A mind in full possession
of its experience", and thinking
of you, of all that chaos is already
repossessing

behind the widening, night-glittering
moat, sometimes I'll rant, sometimes
grieve, but rather now would
sidestep eternitywards and glimpse
a sort of comfort there,

out under the stars where
every human's in soul-motion,
and know the private life's
motley and generous and in its
unwatched manifoldness

may fly finally above ranting
or grief, its soon-surrendered
experience full of destructible small
glories like wings glinting
in odd places

under the eaves, possessed only as
rain over a barn's roof is possessed,
as a book shelters a mind
in its trusted patterns, or as
a thrilled child

laughs even while leaves
resume their pause, shading
pressed grass—
all soon restored to time, things
not important enough

for saving, images it was
sufficient to reflect on
only a little, the briefest glance
towards which may, however,
deliver us.

Landslides

GROUNDHOG TESTIFIES

There is a narrow endless place
where the earth has frozen. On this
they live at unbelievable speeds
while it is light and when it is dark
new ones, ten times longer
and composed mostly of yellow air
the same width as the frozen place,
live there instead; these in spite of
so much greater length behave
about the same. You cannot dig there.
The next day they all come back,
they have not grown tired but have only,
we suppose, discovered their mistake.
Who knows what other purpose
this could have? When we go into
the frozen place they are displeased and
kill us. They are unable to stand,
as we do, motionlessly for minutes erect,
and when being so deprived they grow
distressed or weak they smash one another.
They have no idea how fragrant and far down
home is.

PHOTO

Here I am at fourteen with
my arm in a sling, grinning out
at a world I can remember
looked almost entirely opaque
but not letting on. By the way
this hasn't really changed.
I had fallen off my bike,
that loose gravel at the corner
of George and Wellington—
the arm healed fine. That my eyes
are so intimidatingly clear is what
causes this poem. Into them
have since passed a billion or so
images, not all of which have
ever made it out again:
a girl taking off her clothes
for my sake, doted-on epiphany,
may all such lambencies linger
a while longer—or, other times,
death's dramas or the first leafings
of new-printed pages. Obviously,
eyes become crowded. But here
this gaze is tranquil, intact, it dreams
the unentered houses of my future,
the patiently waiting rooms—
these have been lived in here and
there since, but the photo knows
nothing of that. Below everything
shown here, conjecturally
taking it easy outside the sling,
a familiar, indolent hand.

WALKING IN THE SNOWY NIGHT

You cannot imagine how I long for this creature. I dream
of her every night and wake with my heart all sore.
        —Thomas Mann, in a letter (about Katia, later his wife)

In this softfall of early night snow
this enveloping silence
this soundless drifting-down which continuously
obliterates even while I walk
the proof of my being here,

you cannot imagine how I
long for you.

Among all the exaggerations of art and snow
which veer past me down onto this
snow-narrowed sidewalk, seeming now
in this silence to curtain and shelter me
from my recent life

your imagined voice arrives saying
I love you. Saying *my love.*

I nearly fall down.

Obvious that these were the right sounds
even though they were only imagined—
the knee-deep white track I am following
which seemed about to rock up towards me
now steadies itself kindly.

So I listen again, here it comes, *I love you,*
this time a never-glimpsed panorama
of 'home' hollows me, the roof of the world
down from which all these small irregular

fragments of white softness are drifting
rounds outwards with possibility.
There is nothing here except this undistracting
accumulation of white and these
simple thoughts of you
which I continue towards privately.

The streetlights have just come on.
What an unceasing veering down out of
the dim greyness up there above the lights!

I needed to renew myself like this with silence
and with thinking of you;
by now I have been in this whiteness so long
almost all the dark colours
have withdrawn from me.
How the old perplexing images have
dwindled off into the silence!
The whole shape of my face has changed,
now it understands only its preparation for you.

I must prevent your little subtle breasts from
being thought of
or all this may become less peaceful.

IN THE DREAM OF MY GRANDMOTHER'S TREE

In the dream of my grandmother's tree
little chasms of wind caught my glance
runnelling small eye-roads of leaves
high up there leading into the transparent
heart of things, and I remembered how
strange I used to feel looking up
knowing I would be old sometime and have
no special plans. But then in the dream
a smell of lilac descended
from the tree onto everything and
watchful, unhurried children began to
emerge along the branches, most of them
I had known, especially one who died young
falling from a railing and who was
always patient and smiling when I was
hardly ever, though it is perhaps he
more than anyone who keeps death
open for me—and a tension or pressure
began to be felt, or a tumult as if
just now a very old idea was being
broken into—and mothers and also
some fathers were standing beside me with
eyes looking upwards and calling up saying
This is the way you really always were,
isn't it, not the later way when you were big,
we knew you would be like this because
there has been nothing in the world
we have cared for nearly as much
since! And now one quite near me
called up to a child sitting with his legs
dangling, saying *How could those leaves*
ever have allowed you to pass so unnoticeably
into the angry, darkening distance? But

another said, *Never mind*, and still another said,
It's all right, this is why we are here,
this matters more than anything.

BEHIND ALL OF THESE PLACES IS HAPPINESS

Behind all of these places
is happiness, happiness
drifts there, reliable and unvexed
happiness.

It is behind the false wife who
shrieks in the house while
the true wife rises from the crystal pool
in the woods and the hyaline beads
of water shake from her
blameless white body as she
walks through the still-uninvented
years towards him.

And it lies behind
the vast foggy plains
where the horses wander freely.

And happiness lies within
the dying man whose journeys
and harbours and landing-strips
will be of no interest to anyone now,
they are about to become as complete
and invulnerable as poems.

And it lies in
the tremendous dark nights of the countryside
where naturally no one will look for it
where nothing at all has ever been found.

And it lies in watching
TV with his wife. As he says, "Especially
the travellers' tales from abroad. We like those
best. The tribes of people far away."

And it lies in the clearing
you passed through when you were young
when the way the grass blew a little towards one side
stopped all other thoughts and
everywhere around you
things were so obviously about to become words;
though your memory's way back
to this clearing is overgrown
like an old road.

And happiness lies between
the legs of a woman
I dreamed sincerely of
only a couple of nights ago.

And it can lie in imagining
you are your own great-grandfather
and living safe as he did,
with everything all settled.

And also where the knight waits
in his black armour
on his black horse
in the glade beneath the alder tree,
his unseen face beneath its visor is
patient and enchanted with happiness.

Yes, in all these places
is happiness,
and in some other places, too.

ALL CHANGE

Give me back my little girl in California
this old woman thinks, watching the tely for about
half of the many years since that one grew up and
got married and flew away

For my young heart's humiliation, Seigneur, be
glorified, this fellow praises under his breath,
studying the disappointing lineaments of a once-haughty beloved's
much-forwarded inquiring photograph

What a lot of those squally days at the cottage I would gladly
endure,
just one more climbing between your adored perfectfit thighs,
some extra minutes with my dad who will pause and turn towards
me from
his job of thinning out the cedar hedge,

she or he years too late ruminates

but I
watch my small son lean forward onto his left skate
to bend around the far curve of the rink, and know that
on our walk here from the house next winter he will not reach out
for my hand, dangle it near though I may

and I cannot approve of this, this cries out piercingly for remedy

he coasts by smiling long before I can figure out what to do

"My sin was too much hope
of thee, loved boy", noted
Ben Jonson when his six-year-old
fell out of the world

before anybody could notice, being
too slight at that age
to be got a good grip on,
and so it has been with

many a new one, they fall
clean as whistles
down from their own still-future-misted
accomplishments, leaving

among other unelaborated scenarios
the odd somewhere-budding
sensational girl to put, probably, up
with lesser caressers. And

everywhere unmodified and undiminished
from the dispersed little huddlings
which once stood about staring down into
unassimilatable holes

in one or another sacred flattened meadow
where mossy headstones still show clues
to the lost and buried treasure (and still
record the dates

these ships sailed away—imagine! how
could they? sailed away!—) issue cries
too unappeasable to bear thinking of,
audible fragments of which

may still reach us, complaining of
these small persons continuing to resolutely
file down into the earth although
utterly forbidden to do so

(even worse, this, than staying out
in the rain or wearing your new shoes
into the playground—*Wear what you like!*,
 or, remembering, *Liked!*)—

yes, it goes on still, you would think that
the little grief-rises dotting these meadows
would by now have mollified whatever or
whoever it is,

some unpictureably vile beast obviously,
and up they'd be allowed to come, bursting
with millennia of jammed-together
images of being thought about,

for instance that man standing
all by himself in the hot noonday
out there on some city's sidewalk,
lifting a hand in

a wide gesture although no none is
near and no one watches his gesture
(it is for you, little one, he is
conversing with dead you),

or that woman who is thinking
ridiculously of how she was allowed
to measure your height against
the doorframe

only those few years; and here,
for there is always one like this,
"a reader," here is one reciting
old verses which ask

Wer reitet so spät
Durch Nacht und Wind?
and answer, *Es ist der Vater*
Mit seinem Kind

Who rides so late
through the night so wild?
It is the father
with his child

and Death calling softly
from either side
will steal his darling
from the dreadful ride

—O, the children should pop up
into the air out of their potent
places, even though they are
still perplexed by

all this, by these far-too-long
mother-and-father broodings which have
now forced them to reappear, and
the rooks perched

in the high branches of the thin-leafed
beeches, always so heat-and-rook-filled
where these things seem
to take place,

will fly up
calling, calling, calling, calling
and everything starts now
just as it started once before but

stopped.

OLD SUNKEN SHIPS

The modesty of them! An hour's flashy hubbub
and then such endless disavowal,
such embracing of failure, only
ribbed sand in shadowy re-establishings and
little frills of water wrinkling
here or there in docile far-downness.
They are like dreams redescended, like
the averted limbs of lovers (sated
though soon again perfect), like
children tumbled below memory.
And where they meant to go
years of everything have not happened.

He let go of my hand
and I was lost
said the damp-eyed girl in
the film version of 'Zhivago'

—she was dimly remembering
her father, forever missing
among a crowd of extras
during the Revolution—

and although I wasn't really
much involved with her or
her feelings of love and loss,
still, the mine-shaft opened,
her lines sped down and something
felt familiar and right about it,
way down there as it was.

He let go of my hand—

It is not I, it is the child I was
towards whom the dark shaft
blooms. And I may grow damp-eyed
if I choose.

The garden swing sways on its
heavy rope, slightly, in a skewed motion.
That child is just turning away,
he believes this will still be
serious tomorrow.

He thinks about something interesting
by the scuffed wall next to

the flowerbed. Time leans close,
it will obliterate this. It will raze
first his interesting thought
and then the way the coolness
of the day breathes in under his thought—
the way it exhilarates a little the passages
of his thought as he stands here.

In the blue morning before
anyone else is up
every object he sees is strange
and grave. A clean fork
on the kitchen table
has survived the night—
it is unaccountable
as the moon. Over there is
an unguarded plate. Should he guess
that as he sees these things they are
becoming immortal?

He is becoming immortal too,
and opaque—

   —unless—unless I reach out
and take his hand.

I will reach out.
I will take his hand.

What will happen to us both then?

THE POLAROID MEMORANDUM

One of our agents files a mixed report
on the transfiguration of the world

I am pleased to advise that
more and more are in sanctuary.
Shunning the body's shiver and
the disappointments and griefs
of unreliable day, men and women
arrange themselves hourly
for my inspection. Chaos
attends these gatherings, the men
and women murmur admonishingly
to ward it off. They hope their
settled faces will subdue it. Their eyes
entreat me, they want me to like them,
and they no longer fear
my brief darkness—
beyond it, they seem now sure, is
a glossy beckoning. So they smile,
holding still as Art. They have had
enough of comings and goings.

For every woman, every man admitted,
one is lost. He stands always
on the other side of safety, watching.
He stands so I cannot see him.
Sometimes he cries out, naturally
no one answers. At most they
adjust their stillnesses. They can sense
they are almost there. They are tense with
joy, they are inexorable.

He does not understand.

He remains as he is, unsheltered.
One imagines him despairing, anxious,
at times I have thought he is offering
himself, scapegoat and martyr, atoner,
God's frisker. Though more likely
he has merely not grasped what is
happening. Their moment of *kairos*
come, those others hurtle into
serenity and stasis,
they attain their final form. Time
withdraws from them, it has
nothing more to do with them forever.

He is not among them. Searching
among those faces and little shiny
attitudes, you will not find him.
He is omitted. Mutability
has claimed him. He has gone back
out of plausible sight, he has stepped
into the currents of rooms,
you cannot count on his face enduring.

He has retreated into savagery.

It is not easy to report this.

somewhere far from this comfort
ah, far from this,
myself, it is my old self
far from here

such luck to be glimpsed there
I am in a field, a field
or it is instead my childhood
and not a field

but even to be glimpsed there
to be caught sight of at the last minute, perhaps,
before it is too dark
for a field, or for childhood

I turn my head, my head
and light moves over the field
I am like a lighthouse
turning my head

the light runs far off
swiftly over the fields
it lights up what was becoming all dark
lights the stretches of swift dark land

there I am there, right there
for a moment in the light
Oh, I am sure it was I
as the light ran over me

what was I doing, doing
I seemed to be reading , or
talking, perhaps, talking
yes, words and light together

the words seemed like fields,
fields, but the dark entered them
almost at once, those words,
they filled up with darkness instead

it had hardly left them, the dark
and there it came again
so they had practically no chance
only for a moment in the light there they were

and now I am gone, or
preoccupied, yes, preoccupied
the light passed beyond me
while I was preoccupied

it ran ahead over the fields
they are empty of me now, they are only fields
though the light ran over them
anxious and swift as childhood

K. in Love

A thought of you
Overwhelmed me. I looked
Out the window. For relief?
I don't know.
The sky was grey.
This is how things are with me.

Showing so much need
Frightens me. I should
Block the door against
These pages' leaving
Rather than let anybody read them.

It's so lonely here
Without you. I try
To write cheerfully and
Every word on the page
Bursts into tears.

What a privilege, though, being allowed
To write you! The abominable world
Grunts just off the page
But can't get in. Your gaze
Which will fall on this
Is a fire keeping it off.

Now is your chance to
Tear this up unread. Right now!
But there's this earlier *now,* too—
My chance not to write it.
I've already lost that one.

I'm always writing to you
At night. So it's always
My night-face looking down
At this page. And then your
Day-face reads it. No wonder
There are difficulties !

I try to let ordinary cheerfulness
Or uneasiness take over, but the world is
Breathing so close to me now that
Intermediate modes like those
Don't have a chance.

Being unfaithful to so many years
Is certainly nothing to be
Proud of. All my own past
Gone watery. But people wouldn't
Blame me if they could see me
Leaning out from my wan life watching you
Ripple in the sunlight.

I was with a few people the other night
And made some lighthearted remarks
About you. Anybody would think
I cared about you only
To the usual degree. But
Every time I mentioned your name
I was holding onto the table.

Without you these lines obviously
Wouldn't exist. Also, however,
Writing them is what allows me
To exist without you. If I could
Rely on this lasting I'd just
Write on swiftly through the nights
And hardly miss you.

Until you, life was
Such a comedown, I used to feel.
How did I know?

I opened your letter as if
It was just a letter,
And then your photo fell
Out. Since then I've been
Thinking about you even harder,
As if among all those
Extra images of you that I'm
Thinking into being
You yourself will accidentally
(Even if you weren't considering coming at all)
Appear.

Strange that a photo falling
Out of a letter could change
All my words—not just the ones
I've been using to think of you with.
If you yourself fell among my new words,
No matter how many of them happened
To be there, they would know
Exactly how to arrange themselves.

Thanks again for that photograph.
Now when I have to go anywhere worrying
I take your picture with me
And lay it on the table
Beside me. I nonchalantly
Put my hand on it
When I speak. When I'm keeping quiet
It's enough to just look at it.

It's lucky your parents and sister
Aren't in the least concerned with
My boring tastes. They'd resent
Being marched out of this
Family photograph you sent me,
One after another and quite
Unceremoniously, until
Only you were left. Especially
If I then came in and leaned towards you,
Fainting with happiness.

Everything that I ever imagine happening to us
Happens in a place
Nobody has ever mentioned.
Through not ever being mentioned
It has stored itself up.
It has become just as interesting as
Dreams or long journeys or dying.

In every look I get from you
There is some place beyond my reach.
When I consider this I wonder
How I ever came close to you
At all. However, although I
Cannot imagine myself being
In any of those places, if I *were*
I would think it was wonderful, and
I would do various small tasks,
Not changing or improving anything
But being very happy.

How often I feel this: that you
Are turning your face
Towards someone who doesn't
Deserve to see it, who sees it
And goes on just as usual. As if
That Trojan prince had arrived back home saying
No, there was nobody special.

It's a shame my feelings about you
Rushed straight at me and then onwards
So fast, making me race to keep up.
Why couldn't they have come more slowly
So I could still be noticing myself loving you
More each day for a lot of unimportant but
Freshly-discovered reasons? For instance
The way you allow the sleeves of your pullovers
To intrude over your wrists and even, sometimes.
A little over your hands. But things like that seem
Already understood.

Such a long time until I'll see you again!
If I tried to write down exactly
How long it will be, despair would fall frighteningly
On my writing hand
And on all the weeks in between.
So I lie about it. I write
We are meeting in the park in a few minutes.
Now I wonder if I dare write
The sun is shining benevolently all over the park.

Here's the latest on us,
Vouched for by my own lying hand.
We walked in the park in the sunlight
For two hours. Three. I noticed
You smiled frequently when I spoke your name.
... Having written that, I'm now
Curious to know why you smiled
So frequently. But I won't ask just yet.
Such caution! It's come too late, however,
Because even beginning to think about asking
Has just altered your expression to
A far-off look.

When you refer in today's letter
To "our love", completely new images of home
Drift near. Out of this driftstuff issue
Voicesounds of kindness,
Your speechless legs
Almost all the way up, and I think
Piano music.

I imagine you sleeping and
All the shadow-images crossing and re-crossing
Behind your closed eyelids. Obviously
These are people wanting to be
Stored to one side or the other.

When I'm sitting about indecisively and notice
Objects like a chair or a rug close by, their
Certainties nearly efface me. This typewriter,
For instance, is so much surer of itself than I am:
If it ever has second thoughts about anything,
a superfluous line-blurring adjective, say,
 its keys move once or twice and that's it,
finis, done. If *I* could be more like that—!

A girl was visiting us last night who
Reminded me of you, so I watched her
As closely as she'd let me. When I'd
Tracked down every bit of you
That was there, I went out for a walk
So I could think about those bits.

Going for long walks by myself is
Something I've never done much of before,
Boredom soon turned me homewards.
But now fear and love make me
Fly down the sidewalks.

I'm struck silent by
Your mysteriousness in this photo.
An average person like me
Should not presume to probe into
Such depths—standing close
Should be all he's allowed.

Though perhaps—what do you think of this?—
Standing close to such depths,
Even if you don't understand them,
May still be the best way of understanding them.

So this is how it was!
A photo of you as a little girl
Looking out from your twelve years
As if you are saying
I am withholding most of myself
From this photo for some reason
Connected with the future—

I walk towards that little girl
Though never ceasing to look over there at
The grownup you. I'm not sure
This is the right way to behave but
What I would like best would be if
That little girl would lead me
Right up to you and introduce us, but doing all this
Slowly, so that by the time we were
Beginning to like each other, she would be
You, or almost.

I have put all your photos into an album.
Now its sleep's uneasy—its dark pages
Aren't used to dreams like these. But at least
My room has regained a little composure.

Whatever happens between us now
I think about for hours,
Until it changes me.

This one's just for me: *your naked*
White breasts. I know I shouldn't
Write that, it's self-indulgent. But
Since it's just for me I can write it
Any way I like, there's no call to be
Original—which very often, I think, only means
Moving the main words off their centres.
Anyway, I've now brought these words
Onto this page. I feel like Prometheus,
Bringing breasts to man. But really just
Yours, and just to me.

My body keeps on doing whatever it has to
But my thoughts only link up with it
When it's with you. That's when
Little pieces of future start
Floating together and I have even begun thinking
It might not be too late to make
A whole life
Out of the bits I started out with quite a while ago
Or have added on here and there since.

How sad I used to be before I met you, knowing
Nobody in the world had me in her thoughts
When she woke up in the morning,
Or paused by her window at night.

So often I have so much to say to you
That it's like a roomful of people
All trying to get out at once through
The same little door. This page, for instance—
How inadequate! It's as if I had to
Look at you through it and my eyes
Feel too far apart to do that, or as if
It's an escape-hatch which not even
My first mouthful of greetings
Will ever fit through. And all this is
Nothing compared to the geographies
My thoughts about you pretend they need.

But how will I ever attract your attention
(Or keep it once I've got it) when we're
Living together? If you should glance
Towards the door, the hall beyond it would
Unsettle me all afternoon, and lowering
Your head onto your arms would
Efface me altogether.

When we're together I jabber away
About everything imaginable, telling you
All sorts of things about myself.
But when I leave
These things all race after me,
They can't wait to fit themselves back inside
In exactly the same order they were in before.
So I'm as unknown as ever.

So many more images of you
I'm left trying to incorporate
After every time we've been together!
They crowd in and everything else has to
Clear out at speed: even this room I'm
Sitting in and writing to you from
Has just this moment fled into the past.
If I could tell you how much I long to
Run my hand over this old wooden table-top
Which my forearms, puzzling out poems,
Have warmed late at night for years!
But right now it's a little insubstantial.

Another example. You said "I love you"
Without giving me any advance warning about
The space this would need, and right away
Such image-storms flew that all my memories
Ceased, or seemed to pause, or were suspended,
For a while—long enough for me to realize
How it would feel if they quit permanently.
The sense of newness and of being perfect
Was exhilarating, but probably nobody should be
As unfaithful to the years as that.

How do you feel about
People who don't want to be
The way you think they are?
When we met and of course I instantly
Fell in love with you
I realized I would have to change into
A quite different sort of man
In order for you to love me.
But you left a few minutes later
Before I had time to change.

I have just realized that
I love you even more than I thought.
I was re-reading a poem called
The Owl by Edward Thomas and
After the lines "the bird's voice,
Speaking for all who lay under the stars,
Soldiers and poor, unable to rejoice...".
I happened to think of you, and realized
I love you as much as I love those lines.

So then without losing any time
I subjected you to a further test,
Which was "Forests reign over the past".
You are just as beautiful and sad as that, too.

Think if by some accident we now
Forgot each other, how would
Our huge uncompleted feelings
Ever find enough to do in the world?

There must be enormous areas of pressure
Like huge dim balloons
Bobbing around in different places,
The result of deaths of
People who didn't finish explaining
How they felt about somebody.

Of course it's far from necessary
To die in order to quicken
This sensation of unfinished business.
I have a lot of previous selves,
Most of them dissatisfied, who think
Everything they have ever felt
Is only a first draft of what they could have felt.

Here come my latest marks on a page
Looking up at you. So frail—
How can I expect them to accomplish anything?
Nothing alive is so weak.
Your opening the envelope has
Dazed them, it's because of
The light flooding in.
At least wait till they recover.

PIcture me pressing language out of
Loneliness. Words always appear
And it's still me who decides which ones—
Only sometimes they won't lift their gaze.
When this happens the letter just
Stands there facing inwards and I never know
Whether to send it to you or not.

Everything you show me of yourself conceals
Years and years of things beneath it. Seeing your arm
Lingering on the rolled-down car-window a while ago
I found myself thinking of when it was in high school
And used to linger, probably, in a similar way
(Of course I was too far off then to notice it,
And it was a different car and everything).
I don't mean that you need to show me things like that, though
Mentioning's enough.

This has gone so far that
I deliberately put things near you
So you'll pick them up or look at them
And then this process is bound to
Start happening. It's as if in this illicit way
I'm trying to recover your whole life.

If we both take a long look
At something and then stop,
It goes off with our two looks in it.
What this will mean *sub specie
Aeternitatis is:* very little. But
It's nice to think about.

Being by the sea last weekend was important.
The time spent walking with you maintained itself,
It neither sank nor rose, only the sea
Beside us was doing that—
I was happy feeling we were passing
The great test of the sea.

Behind us and those seaside crowds we walked among
Our hotel room waited, apparently understanding
It did not belong to anything there,
It was an exception to everything.

In fact, do feelings such as
We have for each other
Belong to the content of a life?
Surely they are exceptions
To life's content?

Plenty of people have *Doppelgänger.*
I just dreamt I met yours
In Cairo, with your face
The colour of twilight. You said
People had no obligation to fulfil
Obvious emotions, but that this
Wouldn't be a problem.

Another dream. I stand looking down
At the Limmat from a bridge in Zurich.
Photographs of our earlier selves
Flutter down into the Limmat's little waves
Which flow in a regimented way beneath the bridge.

Final dream. This is certainly
Connected with the Zurich dream.
Freud says to me: "The unconscious mind
Has only a few characters to play with."
You aren't there but wherever you are
You avert your face—this is your way of
Showing that you are thinking of a comment
You will soon make. Then another photo
Falls into a little wave and is borne off.

What a nice feeling it is
Carrying these sealed envelopes to the mailbox
And then walking home again afterwards.
There's such a goodhearted fellow gone off
In each of them, who will come into your house
With every word decided, and without having
Looked at anybody along the way.

I send you a last embrace
And now for another interminable day
Am alone. Well, not just yet.
I don't see why I can't
Write again in a few minutes.

LITTLE BIRD

You will not meet
Achilles' ghost,
nor Aeneas'; nor greet
others from that host

of those
who rose
straight up the tower
of their own lives

and, still shining, died
then. (Enviably, to us below—
or else poets, needing them, lied
to make them seem so.)

Who cares? Not you,
I think, who
took little pleasure in such
flamboyancies, and not overmuch

in language, either,
never using two
words when one would do,
and sat in spreading

silence when I, a schoolboy
then, swarmed among syllables
for the sheer joy
& hell of it, monologuing

at mealtimes like an anointed
asshole until, too late,
you'd dispatch me with a pointed
"That's it. Just take your plate

with you when you go, all right?"
It was usually all right. In my heart I
knew I had offended
only against Sparta,

the sort of town
anybody in his right mind
agreed ought to be put down
—nothing but reticence & blind

loyalty and life-minus-wit—
so no hard feelings. Still,
old Spartan, as starts go it
was a crappy one. "Ominous",

I could and will say—but not you,
right? Unexpected adjectives meant
showing off, isn't that so? Well,
at least the problem was evident

early on. Wherever my callow dreams
were headed, you could soon tell
it wasn't towards you;
and at once you fell

into a great patience
with my growing-up,
as if now that I
was reneging on my

little-boy announcement
that I'd have, one day,
a desk beside yours
where we'd work away

side by side until we were old,
there was no hurry anyhow—
none, ever, for anything.
You never told

me so, nor gave me one of your
sidelong, lidded glances,
but now that it's up to me
to decide how

things were, that's my
story. Sorry,
if it's wrong.
Not long

afterwards appears
the banality *dorée*
of my very earliest
European wander-years,

so characterized
because that's how
they swim up towards me whenever
I remember them now:

trite, as they were bound to be,
and embryonic, single-celled maybe,
or just possibly
spermatozoic, their tiny tails

lashing (that innocent-abroad
face inside a frame,
those jejune poses,
but all the same

& even on that clichéd ground
glowing, numinous . . . must have been
the goldleaf surround).
And of these

I sang. Bullshit. Not 'sang'—
semaphored. And only when I was
in the mood. Aerograms,
postcards, and the years going by—

> *Canti, e cosí trapassi*
> *il piú bel fiore*
> *dell'anno e di tua vita* *
> —so wrote Leopardi,

> and I loved those lines
> more than any others
> in the world, probably still do—
> and aged 22

---

* You sing, and so passes / the loveliest flower / of the year and of your life.
    –from *Il Passero Solitario*

loitered on the bridges
of the Arno
reverently mouthing them
like a re-cycled *solitario*

(but it won't do,
you can't write
like that anymore,
can you?)

—much to my
surprise
five
years & then

ten
and several more too
before I was through,
notes to you

from those towns
I walked among
after the tourists had gone,
though not after that song,

no, the song still went on . . .
Basta. Who'd have thought
there would be singing for you, father,
who couldn't carry a tune

across the road? Not
me—though this is meant
to be such. Well, never mind.
Weitermachen.* I still sent

off my signals, newsblips,
whatever—(term-reports on my dream
of an incredibly sophisticated
craft-apprenticeship

such as only the budding young-*magi*
of *Mitteleuropa* had ever got
permission to enroll in until now,
Mann & Musil and that lot,

but now there'd be
me too, why not,
gearing up to
dazzle the anglos)

---

*carry on

so somewhere in the airstream
borne remorselessly back westwards
towards you there was always
that flotsam of

yips from the ancient parapets,
including the odd *cri de cash,* the whole of it
slowly rotating high over
the possibly-brooding

Atlantic to eddy to its final rest
on your small-town
Ontario
desk

(incongruously, I've always
thought. Not that you
didn't deserve to be told
what was up

with me, or at least a sanitized
précis thereof—& not,
either, that I wasn't old
enough to know

I owed you an unrefundable lot.
It's just that, you know,
your laconic desk, my ornate stuff
arriving to haunt it,

how badly, ever,
did you really want it?
There must have been days
when you'd gladly

have let that cup
pass from you. i.e.,
viewed as a cup
it was up

to me to take a good
look at what I was offering. *Contents*,
know what I mean? Well, I soon would.)
Now here's a break

in the action, old sacred
father. Last night I
dreamed of you. In the midst
of this journey

of our poem, I found myself
in what seemed the great hall
or nave of some quite
ancient pile, all gloom

and foreboding. At one end was
a walk-in fireplace big as a room,
 its floor deep in grey-&-white
ash, the ash also old.

It was very cold.
There had been no fire
and nothing else warm there
for a hundred years. I saw

a little bird with ash-pale
feathers and ashen, downy breast
picking its way stiffly,
slowly, as if

it had been there forever, over
the white humps of that
soft, ashy plain. Now and again
it would peck

at the ash. Its silence and its air
of absorption, its indifference
to my being there,
were very worrying—

I don't know why this was so,
but the dream knew.
When I lifted my eyes I saw
you in a queue

in a sort of side-aisle,
smaller than you ever were
in life, quite small,
and skinnier

even than you were when you got
so sharp-kneed near the end,
wearing a frayed
though clean white shirt

quite unlike the sort people bought
you at the last, when they'd
decided you wouldn't
notice, no, this was

one of those fine
Egyptian-cotton handmade
nonpareils such as you liked
& had a rack of

(I found three the day
after the funeral, at the back of
your closet; needless to say
they fit me

so I wear them, well-used
at collar and cuff as all
of them are; I think
I like them as much as

you did.) You were as small
as your own father was when he
was old. I put my arm
around you, and you said

you were sorry I had stayed away
from Canada for two weeks. I
knew it had been fourteen years,
which is probably why

I woke up then,
I suppose my eyes couldn't
manage both sleep and tears
simultaneously. What

at some putatively more profound
level the dream means, I'll omit.
It brings me, though,
that bit

closer to what I seem to need to do
next. Which is: build some kind
of bridge towards you,
try to find

a shared place—some place where
if I could, at last,
just not offend, just let
an hour or two tick past

in mild observings
of the untroubled air, say,
the agreeable time
of year, or day,

before I made
my inevitable gaffe,
you know, *chattered,*
some sublime

probably nervous
probably manic
rush of cleverness—
well, if that would be

a place we could make it to,
then it's a start,
right? And if the longed-for
heart-to-heart

followed, *great.* As they
say. But may I just add this,
fast & undecorated,
without losing

your attention? *Making us*
whole, father, is what
all this seems to be about.
"Sounds very grand,"

I hear you say—
the sort of remark without
which we conceivably could
have been much closer, by the way—

but let that pass, who
cares, *merde, I* do, I always did,
except that this time
you didn't really even say it,

did you?—and so, unoffended
(let's *both* be, OK?), or
only a little offended,
I'll reel on:

*& any aspiration
 to whole-
ness is going to
have to mean,*

*granted who
the two
of us
are,*

a kind of
binding of
silence
& language

together: a making of
one thing out of us two,
and I do not know
how to do

that. It is
a myth-size task,
father, ask anybody.
Ask

Wittgenstein,
it was always more
his sort of thing
than mine.

Wovon man nicht
sprechen kann, darüber
muss man schweigen. *
After which

_____
* That of which one
  Cannot speak, of that
  One should be silent

Wittgenstein complicated it.
Yes. Well, up to him, we
mustn't mind. What we find,
fast-forwarding

past all that,
is you wearing discretion's
old-tyme hat
& me, as long ago,

cavorting—
how many lunches I missed
doing that antic stuff
when I was small!—I

wouldn't have a glimmer
against you now at all. I
mean, think about it: that
incessant stir

of words vs. your *(leider!)* *
High Noon stare,
mountebank vs. shy
buckskin rider—

---

* *leider* = 'pity,' as in the French *dommage*. The German word used here has,
of course, the advantage of rhyming with 'rider'.

it's a blatant mis-deal,
father, entirely obvious
who's villain and who gets, silently,
to star in the last reel

here, so cease, quit
find a new role,
I advise myself—
and, "if only it

were that easy," is what
drones back.
No: there's only one track
remaining that might,

repeat *might,* lead out of here,
past the leaf-babble &
the restless, head-high sumac
all of us in this land

linger to listen through,
all of that illegible, unechoing,
opaque Canayjun unhistory, and
it's this:

if silence is what's
perpetual here, dark bough
we're always led to
when we're young,

& keeps us (having showed
us nothing but the thicket
of itself, no road
to old descended cities

or palimpsest of archaic
human murmurs here
at all) innocent and safe
as long as we stay near,

then what if I,
no longer young and even though
it knows I'm not its ally,
invite it in? in among

all these embellished insect-cries
of mine, my 93 (so far)
stanzas of tries
to rhyme you back

in from the mute & maybe
sacred wood I think of you
always walking in now,
needless to say

not talking in but
walking in—? . . . I
could invite it in, sure, or
while I'm at it try

to call forth spirits
from the vasty deep, why
not, but would it or
would they

come? . . . Father,
listen as hard as I can
for those silences
in your woods

and in your life,
obiter non dicta of a man
for whom "happiness," "wife,"
"glad/sorry

to hear that"
represented the apparently
entirely-adequate outer signals
of that inner human journey

—well, "Christ!"
is what I'd once have said,
& sometimes did (you had
to *be* there,

often) but will not now. Instead
I'll try to show us, bind
us, this way. I,
off in the towns

your patience bought me,
casual spendthrift of
a frame & gait
so much like yours

it seemed a too-punctilious fate
had stamped our immoderate
pattern twice, find
myself strolling

the heat-stilled
grandes allées in
those unforgotten,
glance-filled

afternoons so oddly
within your gift
(such innocent giver!
such ambivalent

gift!), collecting scenes
and silhouettes and
now and then quick, crowd-subduing
incandescings

of faces I'll
dream of until
I'm old
(so compellingly dream

that nobody,
here's a promise,
will ever be told
more than this

parenthesis),
meantime arranging language
on a page, too much of it
still noisy, obvious,

servile to the age
and for an apparently interminable while
caught in a cage
of ego and insecurity

. . . but then haltingly, spasmodically,
random end-runs at first, beginning
to make it the hell out of there,
early feints

in the direction of a subtler
place, for instance taking
that extra half-or-whole night
over a line, over

only one line, and eventually,
close to pale morning,
realizing just how much
light

you could actually stack
onto an image,
unshadow a face
with, unpack

out of e.g. some night-
felled street . . . in
brief, replacing or
trying to replace

all that used to be
or that I could by now
identify as being
easy, clever,

narcissistic, tame,
with Flaubert's intolerable
requirement: "Every word
tipped with flame"—

. . . Unnecessary to tell *you*, sir,
I didn't always pull it off.
      (Little joke—
father or *hypocrite lecteur*,

at most there was occasional smoke.)
But enough of apprenticeship
matters. I wrote, re-wrote, wrote
again, stuff

nobody ever read,
lived as the sages advise us to live,
unnoticed, making my wants few,
slept in the little alcoved bed

by the Mälar-sea in Stockholm
alone or not but
hardly ever thinking of you,
hardly ever caring where,

in any caring way, you were,
only assuming you were there
because you had always been there—
. . . And there, of course, you were,

minding the storehouse of yourself:
guarding your tree,
your pond, your renewable
gravel drive, trajectory

of your life's imagery,
all bas-relief and in one place
like some rain-
obliterated god-face

& no noisier.
(To say more
about this will be hard.)
(Yet I must go on. *Oedipus, II, iv.*)

So, more.
Nothing persuades us so absolutely
a man's stinking at the core
than virtue's white-lit facades—

and you flickered, yes,
in the small-town night,
not showily but reliably, a beam
to walk by and light

a way home. Minus the metaphor,
your honesty showed
what that word meant
and the town owed

you for it. Owed you, O, about
half of all it understood
of civic honour. Which *should*
have boded no good!

    And yet, & yet—
what *should* come next
doesn't. Postmortem siftings
of the subtext

of your life (it was my job:
'executor,' it's called), files,
old papers, tracking through
some of the miles

of onionskin brokers'-receipts,
stocklistings, your on-going
entries in those spacious, wide-margined
ledgers showing

clients' in-&-out share-costs,
in fact the whole arithmetical
tour de force that your
lightning-fast, infallible

multiplications and divisions
stunned me with from day
one to right now .... also, echoes
of old letters (needless to say

these are *to*, not *from*, and include one I wish
I hadn't found from your mother, my Gran,
folded to wallet-size & faded &
counselling you to be a man

they'll be proud of out there,
aged 19 on the Somme) which show
somebody's relief, somewhere,
at having followed

this or that gnomic, I'll bet,
tip from you: plus more than one
extremely terse note intended for
no eye but your own,

notes recording transactions so palpably fair
they are naive, almost they embarrass;
among these, memorably,
a $200 debt

you paid to some Jehovah-smitten
cousin whom *your father,*
for God's sake, *not you,*
had met

out in Alberta & who wrote shaky-handed
and decades later to claim it,
even though obviously
nobody could blame it

on you, who couldn't have known
of it. The point, though, the unusual
(I think) point here is that *nothing*
odd, or off, or unlisted

came lurching out from under a stone,
there was *no* dark image among your *Nachlass**
for a part-time executor to stumble upon—
nothing that lurked

in some furtively visited file or behind, e.g.,
a shelf of unreadable masterpieces.
To half-borrow a phrase, father,
I have seen your past, & it worked.

———
* leavings, testament

So what's to say, old mole—
can'st work i' the stillness a whole
lifetime and leave no stain
or sadly sordid spoor

behind, and I'll still complain
about you?—No. Or, um, a little. Only
it's like this, I think. You're gone,
transitting from the word-shy

to the word*less* without a word,
no deathbed recantations
or last-minute language-fireworks,
no Roman candles lobbing

luminous syllables,
all the long-hoarded word-trove
up off the pillow towards
the expectant, inward-leaning faces,

nothing like that at all—which means, of course,
that that stored-up hoard went with you! Father, this can still
stun me: those billion tiny episodes
you'd been party to

plus the frail holding-pattern they'd been in—
all gone, cindered, every one of them
slipped off the lit ledges
of the world we run around in. Just

like that, irretrievable—which is hardly unique,
I know, people do get old and so a lot
goes with them when they go—but it can still
stun. The echo-less finality of it. The simple

dropping of a curtain. Can stun me, anyhow. Like
a sudden news black-out on a remote kingdom,
an ignored province, you as Azerbaijan, way off there
a life soundlessly foundering. Icarus

falling into the sea in that painting,
and the nearby ship that "sailed calmly on".
Until now it looks, father,
as though

all your years lie heavy on your bones
& sullen (or rich—
I'm not sure which)
with unused modifiers—

years you carried inside you, 89 of them,
like little wrapped stones,
without a single one ever guessing
how it might feel to be taken out

& handed up towards the light
(I mean: some *later* light)—as if
it could still be interesting,
as if somebody, anybody,

might have wanted to see more of it
or just see it properly,as if anybody
might have loved it. Father,
I might have. Oh you, you—

you could have shared just a few,
couldn't you? But nothing
doing. It must be why,
though, at the end,

when the dam burst & that flood,
that 'current', they called it, started
pouring through your mind,
that dambursting blood

overrunning all the unvisited
districts in there so fast that nobody
could get close enough
to help—

(and nobody, father, to tell the truth,
was even sure whether *Help*,
as the adverts say, was really
Wanted)...Well, bloody hell,

father, what sort of opaque testament
was that? . . . And yet it's exactly where
we long ago began, isn't it?
Comedy hour, so-and-so many

wrecked meals at the family table
while we re-enacted our
compulsive, neo-Aeschylean
family fable,

those old lunchtime bouts
centering on language, my certainties
and your doubts:
me on the blatantly

middleclass waste which
a starved vocabulary,
even at mealtime,
was typically the norm of,

you on the probable good taste
which shutting up
represented a high form of.
. . . Yeah. Well,

trouble is that since then
the battle-lines have blurred.
What I knew when I was young
concerning the Word

I am less knowing about now.
(*N.B.* Admirable though trite.)
(*N. anche tu B.** I know.)
To choreograph sight

i.e. image, and sound
in some way that can allow
a reader, mine, let's say,
to turn right around

———
* you also Note Well

in the *mezzo* of the *cammin*
of his life towards that long-abandoned
sunstreamed street
of his childhood

is OK, is better than that, is fine—
to change the metaphor,
it is a diving-bell down
through the hyaline

bands of
azure,
cornflower,
gentian,

those blue-tinted, almost pure
submarine glimpsings
of the secret, drifting self, the one
who was *you*, whom you actually,

unbelievably, *were*—but these old,
mislaid sights which can be
streets or stairs or nights
when your mother

came into your room
to hear you say
now that I may go to rest
in my safe and quiet nest

& then lights
out . . . and which, when they work,
remind you you may still be
a little innocent

in spite of your
2
or
3

victories and your many
screw-ups, and can even,
once in a while, lead
to the opinion that henceforth

you will experience every waking moment
of your life as perfectly as if you are,
 e.g., those first seven notes
of *là ci darem*—. . .

. . . well, like I say,
when it works it's great
but so often there's just no way,
know what I mean? So

often those late-discovered images,
which *must* glint like slow-nursed fires
to bring the vast domains
of childhood

into view again after their
so carelessly-used-up mythic days
are so pitiably
under-imagined,

Dante's and Mandelstam's successors
so rebarbatively ungifted and
staggering under their clapped-out,
flyblown egos all the while

claiming as their own the title 'Poet,'
'*Dichter*' (and confirmed, of course,
in such dimwitted pretension by
the usual clutch

of culture-apparatchiks, media-hosts,
convenors, facilitators, etc etc,
fetid retinue of the insecure and the ill-read
whose tireless aphid-cries

are the source and fountainhead
of an entire nation's view of its Art),
that even the good guys
take your part,

father, and given their choice
of company choose to dwindle,
if they can, away from
that piping rout

and towards you. Better mute,
they feel, and so do I often,
than merely metrically astute.
. . . So what's

all this then?—you've
won, old rain-god, after all?
taciturn bird in your
marmoreal hall,

am I crossing the floor
to join you? As sooner
or later I must, of course—
as we *all*

must, and we all
know it, file into
that deafmute ash-pale hall
when our day's done. And

alright then, yes,
almost a yes—except
for this. Even if all
my instincts persuade

me, now, that words go dark
and silence's tawny shade
shines in oxymoronic light
more bright

with every year
that brings me
unexpectantly
through my thinning world,

still something's unresolved.
I say: this voice
—the only one I'll get—
has failed. (Don't think

this modest! I could add:
"and yours", "and his", "and hers".)
Has any writer yet,
leafing his praised, sad

pages, heard that ineffable cadence
he's laboured or dreamed his years
of words towards? . . . No matter.
(Before hurrying on:

yes, *some* matter.
Their dead names are honoured.
Passons.) So there's
the stacked-up wish

to simplify, and say
because ever since our world
began to testify
against or for

itself, no single cry
or deciphering syllable
has come from such as you,
only & always

from that babbling tribe
I joined so early
and love so little now . . .
so that surely

what's left worth listening
for is not what's said but
what's *not* said, what's
kept, unspent—

—and yes, by God, to say so
tempts! Word-truce! The guns
of language sputtering towards armistice!
One or two late cannon-coughs,

some slow-descending flares,
and then
silence. And
silence. And long stares

at each other, longer than
usual, trying, perhaps, to compensate
for such tranquillity; and then
a restiveness,

a disbelief, a lingering unease at this
laying-down of voices.
But gradually armies of us
assembling in pre-dawn

hush, where only
a bird tentatively predicts
the world's still here. Where,
if we listen, another one

liquidly adumbrates
the only allowed discourse, hypnotic
in this dark garden. Lucid.
Naturally it's exciting,

beyond anything our heart's
old quickstepping need for novelty
could conceive of. Who,
with grateful cries,

would not tear towards that?
And then attend to in a sort of rapture
all the rest of his life?
. . . I! I! I! Happily,

happily, would I live then,
under the *föhn*
that blows from the fen.
Wordless in the soughing

wind. Sure thing, you bet, no probs.
Only, you know something?—
It's a lie. A cheap *frisson*.
It's a good old pose—

to all those
expectations it has not got
a single straight-up answer.
Nor a bent one, neither,

come to that. How *could* it? It
tempts, this absence, lures
with its dream of latency,
its lovely rider leaning

into the voiceless
morning, inviting us away
from our marred lives—
but it's less

than human, or
more, in either case
there is no place
where it can reach out

and touch. "It is the duty of
every human being to communicate,
 & silence is a poor way
of doing that,"

wrote Primo Levi, whom I
love, oh, *loved, would* have
if I had earned the right to,
who leaned, he too,

into a voiceless morning, leaned out
over a deep
stairwell in Turin, in his home,
and then

let
him-
self
down

into the silence
he found there,
there was apparently
enough of it.

And elsewhere too there have been
ill-timed reticences when *any* uttering,
however ill-rhymed
or stuttered,

would surely have been preferable—
for instance I would be glad to know why
there should not be
an unforgettably loud cry

waiting halfway up the throat,
up many throats, waiting to
instigate running footsteps
towards those rooms that are vile

beyond all vilenesses,
sequestered and mute while
a child is repeatedly misused there—
    . . . or

O, many scenes more!—
& most insistent of all,
one whose still-drifting pall
of no-comment

floats in over the fields & barracks
& guard-towers of 8,000,000
inflexible dead, and father, nothing
in all the hours of my life

has taught me the trick
of speaking moderately of this and
so I shall not speak of it but will
leave it, quick.

Just as, a hundred quatrains
ago at least, *you'd*
have left *me*, murmuring "Good, good"
so as not to appear rude

while I was still speaking or reading
my 153rd quatrain, but imperceptibly
assisting the idling, patient
newspaper to again

resume its pride
of place; leaving me
to understand I'd
overstayed

my welcome, that what I'd had
to say was said.
And so, as in those old days
of being little, to bed,

or other place where I could
palely loiter on my own
& make small sound
or none,

and hear no birds that I remember
sing. That's how it was before,
father, is now and evermore
shall be, if art's as long

& life as fast
as rumour says: too late now,
and a bit beneath us, too, to pretend
that at the last some fateful,

handy star can coax *us*
towards a tidier end!
When life's boat touches shore
what's to do, the Stoic asked,

and stoutly answered,
"Get out!"—
and since neither I nor
anyone can shout

a ring of questions around
a wordless spectre of a man
and then expect to see
wordy answers brim

inside it, I'll so
decide it. And
therefore *basta*
la partita*, father,

———
*basta la partita: the game's over

and *Schlüss,* and
yes, THE END, I'll now
"Get out!" . . . Except
p.s., father—

a curious thing. Since
you died, all
the faces you ever
wore for me

have changed. Are these
merely the clever
erasures & easy, pencilled-in
mini-discoveries

this interminable letter's
come up with, new
bits of you
arrowing

back out of old, unreported
days & loosening a few
profiles, turning them
edgier? . . . truer?—

(... *younger?* ... *And did you really,*
as I've imagined, stand in the garden
when we were all away
one day

and look up into that tree
beside the pond, and did
enough of a thought
edge in on you to hold both

that tree, which was not,
you knew, always as
tall as this, and also hold
you, who were not always this old,

and did you, standing there, think
how fast it had all gone, gone
like the aproned man
who sold

bread and cheese at the ball
games at Southside
when you were small
and were there with your dad,

and your dad leaning down
towards you saying
if you could count on
always having bread and cheese

in your life
you'd be OK, and how
you briefly thought
about this and it seemed

right, and so
you bit
in again,
feeling safe—)

—Oh, I know these rhymes
don't do
& haven't done
justice to you,

father, because the times,
all the ones I've guessed at,
are gone and so few
of the true

ones appear here at all—
and of the ones that *have*
returned , *none* are whole—
memory-casualties, I'll say

on your behalf, like the goddamn
Somme—but never mind, what's
clear now is that all the dozens
of deep-imprints

I've ever had of you,
ever since each of us took
his first, by now 58-years-ago
appraising look

at the other, are in flux. They've
moved—no, they *are*
moving, they're still mobile—
you must have

moved, right at the far
end of yourself while
life was clicking shut
on its last image

you must have taken a run at it,
at God knows what,
and so your face
is in transit

still. Little tremorings
& fidgets around the sides
of your mouth,
tiny tides

of skindrift there,
that's what's altered,
that minuscule
a rise & fall—

nothing cataclysmic, I mean
it's just a mouth after all,
going through an after-life
crisis apparently,

and now looking a bit
different. Except that
I find myself not just
watching it

but keeping extra-still
so I can hear what it will say.
Which seems, of course,
paradoxical,

now that you've gone away,
cleared off like Houdini
slipping past
the little hooks

the rest of us eventually
notice ourselves on,
silhouettes pricked out
not by the looks

we've given or *been* given, but
by our lives' casual talk.
So watching your mouth
move this way

is odd, & guessing how
it's trying to say
its lost poems.
Little bird,

I know, I know—
they were never really close
and they strayed too far off,
too long ago—

and you don't approve
of my putting it so—
but if I like it
quite a lot,

a word or a quick cluster
of words, which in this case
I do, then more often than not
I'm going to use it,

or them, aren't I? You
can remind yourself
they're only words. They
know they're not true.

Index of Poems

Signal
EDITIONS

Carmine Starnino, Editor

JOY IS NOT MY PROFESSION Muhammad al-Maghut
(Translated by John Asfour and Alison Burch)
WRESTLING WITH ANGELS: SELECTED POEMS Doug Beardsley
HIDE & SEEK Susan Glickman
MAPPING THE CHAOS Rhea Tregebov
FIRE NEVER SLEEPS Carla Hartsfield
THE RHINO GATE POEMS George Ellenbogen
SHADOW CABINET Richard Sanger
MAP OF DREAMS Ricardo Sternberg
THE NEW WORLD Carmine Starnino
THE LONG COLD GREEN EVENINGS OF SPRING Elisabeth Harvor
FAULT LINE Laura Lush
WHITE STONE: THE ALICE POEMS Stephanie Bolster
KEEP IT ALL Yves Boisvert (Translated by Judith Cowan)
THE GREEN ALEMBIC Louise Fabiani
THE ISLAND IN WINTER Terence Young
A TINKERS' PICNIC Peter Richardson
SARACEN ISLAND: THE POEMS OF ANDREAS KARAVIS David Solway
BEAUTIES ON MAD RIVER: SELECTED AND NEW POEMS Jan Conn
WIND AND ROOT Brent MacLaine
HISTORIES Andrew Steinmetz
ARABY Eric Ormsby
WORDS THAT WALK IN THE NIGHT Pierre Morency
(Translated by Lissa Cowan and René Brisebois)
A PICNIC ON ICE: SELECTED POEMS Matthew Sweeney
HELIX: NEW AND SELECTED POEMS John Steffler
HERESIES: THE COMPLETE POEMS OF ANNE WILKINSON, 1924-1961
Edited by Dean Irvine
CALLING HOME Richard Sanger
FIELDER'S CHOICE Elise Partridge
MERRYBEGOT Mary Dalton
MOUNTAIN TEA Peter Van Toorn
AN ABC OF BELLY WORK Peter Richardson
RUNNING IN PROSPECT CEMETERY Susan Glickman
MIRABEL Pierre Nepveu (Translated by Judith Cowan)
POSTSCRIPT Geoffrey Cook
STANDING WAVE Robert Allen
THERE, THERE Patrick Warner
HOW WE ALL SWIFTLY: THE FIRST SIX BOOKS Don Coles
THE NEW CANON: AN ANTHOLOGY OF CANADIAN POETRY
edited by Carmine Starnino

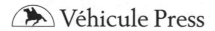 Véhicule Press

www.vehiculepress.com